FRIDAY
MAY 25, 1787

At last! The federal convention has begun. Eleven days late, in the middle of a downpour, twenty-nine delegates from seven states—a quorum—finally got down to business in the State House. They accomplished just one thing today, but it was crucial: They elected a chairman. Robert Morris of Philadelphia, one of the richest men in America, made the motion.

"Gentlemen, by the instruction and in behalf of the deputation of Pennsylvania, I have the honor to propose George Washington, Esquire, late Commander in Chief, for president of the convention."

Washington will make only one formal speech here, but the delegates don't need his wisdom as much as his presence. The General is the most admired man in America. He is the symbol of everything this new nation wants to be: virtuous, respected, honorable, and successful. The General's fate and honor are now on the line here at this convention. So is the fate of this young nation. . . .

About
the Author:

BILL MOYERS IS one of America's most respected journalists and the recipient of just about every major award a broadcaster can receive. He was a CBS correspondent and senior analyst for the "CBS Evening News." Moyers was also the executive director of the highly acclaimed public television series "Bill Moyers' Journal," and previously served as editor and chief correspondent for "CBS Reports." Moyers then returned to public television with a roster of new public affairs projects and with a new independent production company, Public Affairs Television, Inc., which is based at the New York area public television station WNET.

MOYERS: REPORT FROM PHILADELPHIA

The Constitutional Convention of 1787

Bill Moyers

BALLANTINE BOOKS • NEW YORK

The broadcasts of *Moyers: Report from Philadelphia* were made possible by the Corporation for Public Broadcasting, public television stations, and **PaineWebber.**

Library of Congress Catalog Card Number: 87-17421

ISBN 0-345-36160-1

Manufactured in the United States of America

First Hardcover Edition: November 1987
First Mass Market Edition: November 1989

Back cover photo of Bill Moyers © 1988 by Pete Kredenser

Introduction

T HIS WAS A story waiting to be told—again. The idea came from my friend and colleague Alvin Perlmutter. Al had been the imaginative shepherd of "The Great American Dream Machine," a public television series which twenty years ago blazed the trail for the genre of broadcasts now loosely identified as "magazines." That ideas count, even on television, is an article of faith to Perlmutter—one that had made brethren of the two of us. Now we were discussing ways of bringing the Constitutional Convention of 1787 to life for a television audience. And Al had an inspiration: Why not treat the Convention as a news story? Let's report it for a contemporary audience, he said, using this modern medium to help people today grasp the essence of that momentous summer two centuries ago.

Why not? I had resolved two years earlier to make the Constitution my beat in 1987. Having completed a series of documentaries on recent American history—"A Walk Through the Twentieth Century"—I had discovered a television audience that yearns to understand the present against the backlight of the past. Television is no substitute for books about history, but in its own fashion it can whet the appetite for knowledge of the past and send people to historians in search of more solid sustenance.

"Give me a couple of days to see how it might work," I said to Al. With the help of some familiar books on my shelf and others that I had recently begun to collect, I drafted a sample essay, arbitrarily choosing that day in Philadelphia when the delegates debated whether there should be property qualifications for officeholders in the new American government. I incorporated a couple of excerpts from James Madison's record of the proceedings—editing his eighteenth-century prose slightly for clarity to a modern ear—and I imagined the talents of an artist whose drawings could catch the spirit if not the actual likenesses of the Framers. The draft was necessarily brief, and I was confronted once again with the frustration inherent in the short form of television that I had found so confounding in my commentaries for the "CBS Evening News." Issues are so complex and events—past and present—so difficult to decipher that brevity can be the enemy of understanding. "Beware the terrible simplifiers," Huizinga warned. On the other hand, if one acknowledges the limitations of the form, calls on the wisdom of good friends and associates, and presumes not to be offering the last—or even first—word on a subject, the television essay can honor, clarify, and crystallize an idea or event. The most memorable sentences, after all, are the shortest: "Jesus wept" and "the King is dead."

Something else excited me about the idea. One of my mentors, Burton Benjamin, who worked with Walter Cronkite on a CBS News series about the twentieth century, told me a few years ago that journalists are permitted to explain things they do not understand. The tools of our craft are not limited to reporting the present. There are witnesses to consult (diaries, letters), records to check, comparisons to make, and critical judgments to apply, whether the field of inquiry is the making of the Constitution in 1787 or its undoing in 1987.

2

I had already come to look upon my life as a continuing course in adult education, with the world as teacher and journalism paying for the tuition and travel. I had also realized that if I am excited by discovery, onlookers may be infected, too. The college of experience has no quotas, television can be a classroom without walls, and T.H. White's Merlin was right: "The best thing for being sad is to learn something. That is the only thing that never fails. You may grow old and trembling in your anatomies, you may be awake at night listening to the disorder of your veins, you may miss your only love, you may see the world about you devastated by evil lunatics, or know your honor trampled in the sewers of baser minds. There is only one thing for it then—to learn. Learn why the world wags and who wags it."

Those men in Philadelphia wagged the world, all right, and here was the chance to learn more about them. The nature of television obviously would not permit our plumbing the convention in detail. But I did think its storytelling power might help retrieve the Constitutional Convention from the distance to which it has withdrawn, from the iconography that has enveloped it, and from the ideologies that have exploited it. The Constitution was not chiseled in stone on a sacred mountain. It was talked into existence. Through the give-and-take of debate, men who valued the meaning of words and the power of civilized discussion achieved by reason an agreement on how free citizens could live in society and govern themselves.

The Constitutional Convention, in other words, was a political process, wrought by men aware of conflicting interests and finite possibilities. The British statesman William Gladstone, perhaps in a misguided attempt to be complimentary, once described the Constitution as the greatest work ever struck off by the mind of man. Struck off? No, sir. It was hammered, reasoned, shaped, argued, cajoled, traded, and compromised into being. But take heart from that. Recognizing the Constitution as the product of a political process

3

should inspire us more than if Washington had been Moses, taking dictation from Yahweh. If these men got a republic started through deliberation, then certainly we can keep it going by imagining ourselves their heirs of civil discourse. To be sure, they were an uncommon lot. But we still have available to us the insights and arts they brought to politics in their day: the practical importance of history and experience; the necessity of principled compromise; an understanding of government as a contract between rulers and ruled; the need constantly to monitor that contract and the necessity of revising it occasionally; the value of equilibrium in the distribution of power; a knowledge of human imperfection and skepticism toward its perfectibility; and the importance of civic virtue—public responsibility—in self-governance. This is not the revealed wisdom of demigods. It is the insight of experience, the common sense that time and time again saved the convention from ruinous deadlock. To see them as they were takes the Founders down from those old portraits on the wall, unfreezes them, and opens a dialogue between them and us about what it meant then and what it means now to be an American.

This notion of process kept pressing itself on my colleagues and me. Like the convention itself our reporting was a collaborative affair. The credits are printed here for all to read, yet it is not possible to identify who is responsible for one point or another, any more than we can say which member of the Committee of Style—Gouverneur Morris or another—actually thought of the phrase ''We the People'' or wrote ''the privilege of the Writ of Habeas Corpus shall not be suspended.''

Andie Tucher, Paul Budline, and Lindsay Miller were my partners in drafting these essays, and like me they also burrowed deeply into the journals of the convention and other historical sources. My dear friend and previous collaborator Bernard Weisberger was our chief historian, ably backed up by Richard Bernstein. And, of course, there would have been no reports at all without Ron Hull and Suzanne Weil of public television and Donald Marron and John Lampe of Paine Webber, who joined in funding our enterprise.

Whatever the different contributions and our melding roles, each of us—including our senior producer, Kit Lukas, and our cameraman, Tony Foresta—found ourselves in agreement: These men in Philadelphia did not see themselves as either the end or the beginning of nation-making. The Revolution had promised the pursuit of happiness, not its fulfillment. Now these delegates held out the promise of union, not its guarantee. The Framers saw human governance, including the writing of a constitution, as process.

These reports reflect the process. They tell the story in the present tense. I became a witness reporting from 1787 to an audience in 1987. We—audience and I—were connected to an eighteenth-century event and to a process that continues even now. Letters from viewers make me think many Americans found delight and insight from standing in two worlds at once.

The process by which the delegates themselves reached agreement also solved a problem for me. After deciding that Al Perlmutter's challenge was worthy of risk, I was momentarily daunted by the thought that we would have to sustain interest over four months. How could there be enough drama to hold the attention of viewers? What was the *story* in a room of men arguing for six hours a day, six days a week, for sixteen weeks—all those "talking heads" and no archival film!

Yet the day-to-day *process* of making the Constitution was itself the highest and most illuminating drama, replete with suspense, climaxes, and curtain falls. There was a motley cast—some commanding stars, some walk-on parts, and even some comic relief. There were no outright villains, but there were men of complex motives, fierce ambitions, hot tempers, and uneven talents. I confess to becoming emotionally involved in the debates. I learned to count on Benjamin

Franklin for a frequent helping of shrewd wit; on James Madison and James Wilson for high principles and incisive analysis; on George Mason and Gouverneur Morris for picturesque phrases. Mason became the most complex and compelling figure in my notebook, and if I could talk to but one delegate there, he would be my choice. I yearned at the end to steal away with Edmund Randolph for a stroll on the banks of the Schuylkill, hoping he might divulge the true reasons why he refused to sign the Constitution after introducing its main features. This question provoked a hearty discussion among my colleagues. Was Randolph just playing the clever and agile politician, trying to remain popular in a state where the dynamic Patrick Henry and Richard Henry Lee were already denouncing what the convention would propose? Did he really want a second convention? Was he acting out of conscience? I have already sent for a biography of Randolph; television can motivate readers, you see.

I once had a professor, now deceased, who told his class that the Framers were elitists. He was a Texas populist, and he believed that they had stolen the Revolution ignited in 1776. If he were still around, I might now challenge him. Or at least I would argue that if these delegates *were* an elite, as charged, they were an elite bonded not only by property and position but by a shared reading of the Enlightenment, tempered by the practical experience of politics and war. They thought this new race of Americans could reason its way to a better and happier life, but they were not ignorant of mankind's folly and vice. They speak to us even today not from marble pedestals but from a real world where men read Montesquieu and traded votes, horses, and other men. Nonetheless, they assumed that government gathered its authority from the people, that it should be limited and accountable, and that the document they were creating was in fact a contract to be observed faithfully by those elevated to be temporary stewards of the nation's destiny.

Popular democracy as we understand it did not rank high

6

on their collective list of values. But their commitment to the rule of law was universal and unshakable. Following the debates daily, I heard echoes of the covenant theology of my Protestant ancestors—that God has made a contract with humanity, written in the Scriptures and involving promises and responsibilities on both sides. I thought, too, of the Magna Carta, also a written agreement, between the king and his barons, to define the powers of each: this far and no farther. I was reminded of those colonial charters, which spelled out the agreement between crown and colony—Connecticut was so jealous of its original charter that when the king tried to remove it, the Yankees hid it in a tree that became known as the Charter Oak. And I saw these men in Philadelphia as part of a long train of humanity struggling to define the fundamental manner in which the public authority is to be exercised, and to write it down as law. This they did, and it was quite an accomplishment. Yes, they created a government for white, propertied males, including slaveholders. In so many ways they were time-bound. But they sensed the far horizons. Otherwise, they could not have produced an arrangement so religiously tolerant, so flexible, so accessible over time to ever more generous definitions of liberty. They did not think "We the People of the United States" a phrase whose meaning was settled in 1787. It has taken brave political action and strenuous agitation by citizens—not to mention a civil war—steadily to enlarge its meaning so that others were included. The Constitution was no friend of liberty for all until struggle forced its tolerance of all, but the Framers allowed for struggle. What they tried to put in place was—that word again—*a process* by which change could occur without tearing out the roots of the nation. The trunk sways. The branches bend and break. But the idea holds that "if we make a right use of our natural advantages, we soon must be a truly great and happy people."

In reporting the story of these four months I tried occasionally to fill in the background. We leave Philadelphia from time to time to sample the folk flavors, the diversions and dilemmas of an America beyond the delegates' immediate view. And we quote the men sweating in that State House, using words from their letters and various informal writings and the records kept by Madison and others. Inevitably I found myself answering the delegates, joining in the debates and never fully able to forget that I come from another time and place. I was drawn back and forth between the champions and opponents of centralized government. John Francis Mercer of Maryland made sense to me in doubting that "the People of so large a Continent, so different in interests, so distinct in habits," could ever be satisfactorily represented in one national legislature. Wasn't it true through history that republican governments survived where citizens could be intimately involved in politics? Unfortunately, as time and events would prove, the intimate politics of the local level often were nothing more than a cabal against the weak. Despite their "progressive constitutions," states limited suffrage, kept black Americans in slavery, and treated women as second-class citizens until an aroused national government intervened. James Madison and the other champions of a strong national government have been right. We would have remained a union in name only if this Constitution had not changed in response to a widening vision.

In truth, the Constitution was never exactly what its opponents said it was. Or what its champions proclaimed either. The Constitution is what the law, tempered by public opinion, says it is, or what public opinion, tempered by the law, allows it to be. For all its brevity, it is a complex thing, and while the Framers hoped for stability, they never assigned infallibility to their handiwork. The Constitution is our compass, but the sea is still vast and wild and each generation its own navigator.

As you read, try to hear the voices of these men. Television is not the printed page. In a television essay, emphasis can be suggested by a shrug of the shoulder, an eyebrow raised, a glance out the window. The grammar of television is different. Listening is an experience in itself, which is why I believed it important and exciting at least to try to tell this story in a new medium. The message of that summer's labor is not dated. It still glows with life. Politics matter. Language matters. Reason and argument matter.

We are people born of this event. The debates that shaped it are as relevant as the headlines of the day. So is the moral of the tale. In a work widely read by the men in Philadelphia, the Swiss political theorist Emerich de Vattel wrote this:

> . . . But this Constitution is a mere dead letter and the best laws are useless if they be not sacredly observed. It is therefore the duty of the nation to be ever on the watch that the laws be equally respected both by those who govern and by the people who are to be ruled by them. To attack the Constitution of the State and to violate its laws is a capital crime against society; and if the persons who are guilty of it are those in authority, they add to this crime, a perfidious abuse of the power confided to them.

—Bill Moyers

Monday
May 21, 1787

IT IS 1787. Just eleven years have passed since the American colonies declared their independence from England in this very room. What a moment that was. What an assemblage of men.

Thomas Jefferson, with his flaming red hair.

The Adams cousins, Samuel and John.

Benjamin Franklin.

Benjamin Rush.

Edward Rutledge.

Fifty-six patriots in all, fifty-six rebels:

We declare, that these United Colonies are, and of Right ought to be, Free and Independent States.

They matched their eloquence with courage and cannon. What they declared in this room they won on the battlefield in a war that ended four years ago. They were united then— Revolutionary America was a "body with thirteen hearts." Today America has thirteen heads without a body. The government established under the Articles of Confederation operates with dismal inefficiency. Congress has no power to tax or regulate. There is no chief executive. The treasury is bankrupt. In desperation, some of the country's most notable men have called for a convention to cope with the emergency and delegates are right now on their way to this State House. Their stated purpose is to revise the Articles of Confederation, but some delegates have a more radical purpose. They intend to replace the Articles altogether with a constitution establishing a strong national government with sovereignty over the entire country. George Washington is the symbol of their hopes. The General arrived in Philadelphia early, brooding over his country's troubles:

Thirteen sovereignties pulling against each other, and all tugging at the federal head, will soon bring ruin on the whole.

Those dark fears are shared by many of his countrymen. In letters to newspapers citizens confess their anxieties:

We are impoverished by the continual drain of money from us in foreign trade. Our navigation is destroyed; our people in debt and unable to pay. We are discontented at home, and abroad—we are insulted and despised.

So sentiment grows for a strong national government. But there are formidable odds. These men must try to repair a Union that is dissolving before their very eyes. If they fail, so will the new American nation.

Tuesday
May 22, 1787

DAY BY DAY the delegates arrive in Philadelphia. A local newspaper is already calling this "The Grand Convention." Some statesmen worry that it's more likely to be a grand debacle—the final dashing of those hopes they fastened on revolution eleven years ago when the Declaration of Independence was signed here.

Then the thirteen states had a common enemy in King George III. Now they are at each other's throats. Soldiers from Pennsylvania have fired on settlers from Connecticut. Virginia and Maryland quarrel over who can fish for oysters in the Chesapeake. Some small states have set up borders where customs guards inspect a traveler's luggage. Nine states boast their own navies. Some even talk of leaving the Union for alliances with the Old World. New Orleans belongs to Spain and her ships prowl the Mississippi. To the north, British redcoats camp freely on American soil, just below the Canadian border.

Watching General Washington move about Philadelphia, you would not think him perturbed by all this bad news. He puts on a good public show—dining with old comrades, taking tea with the ladies, chatting with Dr. Franklin. But we are told the General's heart is uneasy. If this convention fails to turn a weak government into a strong, he fears the Union will fall apart.

The General is just fifty-five, but lately he has been feeling old and miserable with rheumatism, and he doesn't say much publicly; his modesty is as true as his valor. Fortunately, there will be younger men here as outspoken as Washington is reticent. Men like Alexander Hamilton. He's only thirty-two, but this young lawyer who was Washington's lieutenant in the war shares his old commander's vision:

> There is something noble and magnificent in the perspective of a great federal republic, closely linked to the pursuit of a common interest—prosperous at home, respected abroad—contrasted to a number of petty states, jealous and perverse, without any determined direction, fluctuating and unhappy at home, weak and insignificant in the eyes of other nations.

General Washington's age is more unusual here than Hamilton's youth. Most of the delegates are in their thirties and forties. Some are even younger. They are the first generation to come of age as free Americans. On the eve of this convention, who can estimate what their work here will mean for the generations to follow?

Wednesday
May 23, 1787

IF IT PROVES as hard to create a government in Philadelphia
as it is just to get here, the delegates to the federal convention
are in for a long and difficult summer. There are so many
stragglers that only four states are yet represented. Three
more are needed before the convention can even begin. The
delay has come about chiefly because traveling in 1787 is a
tremendous burden. For the delegation from New Hampshire, the journey will take twenty-one days, much of it on
rocky trails down the Connecticut River Valley. From the
far-off wilderness of Georgia, the trip is 800 miles over swol-
len rivers without bridges and down forest trails left almost
impassible by recent rains. Just to get here from New York
requires a stagecoach, a ferry, and three days of travel.

This did not prevent James Madison from arriving in Philadelphia eleven days early. Since then he's done little but stay
in his rooming house and scribble, scribble, scribble. Madison is a small man—"no bigger than half a piece of soap"—
but he has an intellect worthy of the Herculean task he has
set for himself. Thomas Jefferson—who is in Paris—has virtually emptied the bookstores of France and shipped them to

Madison for his study of the science of politics. As much as anyone, Madison wants the convention to forge a strong national government. His letters, however, indicate a distinct pessimism:

> *If the approaching Convention should not agree on some remedy, I am persuaded that some very different arrangements will ensue. A propensity towards Monarchy is said to have been produced in some leading minds. The bulk of the people will probably prefer the lesser evil of a partition of the Union into three more practicable and energetic Governments. . . . The nearer the crisis approaches, the more I tremble for the issue.*

Madison's anxiety is shared by many other delegates, and this is partly the result of what happened in Massachusetts last year. A veteran of the Revolutionary War—one Daniel Shays—led an uprising of desperate farmers forced into bankruptcy by debt and taxation. They marched on the county courthouses with rebellion in their hearts and pitchforks in their hands, and they just about overran a federal arsenal. It took the state six months to regain control.

The whole episode was further proof to many of America's leading citizens of the need for a strong new government to cope with the nation's ills, including prospect of anarchy. The uninvited and unseen visitors at this convention will be Captain Shays and his angry mob of farmers.

Thursday
May 24, 1787

STILL NO QUORUM. Still no convention. The delegates are arriving at the pace of turtles. General Washington complains that the delays "sour the tempers of punctual members." And the only New Englander to show up so far, Rufus King of Massachusetts, has sent a plaintive letter back home:

> I am mortified that I alone am from New England. Pray hurry on your Delegates—some personal Sacrifices may stand in the way of their immediate attendance—But they ought not to yield to such Considerations—Believe me, it may prove unfortunate if they do not attend within a few days.

One state that is well represented here is Virginia. Its delegation is a constellation of brilliance, with luminaries like George Mason, George Washington, and James Madison. The Virginians huddle each day for at least three hours to plot strategy for the opening session, whenever that might be. In the meantime, there is much in this city to oblige the taste and curiosity of those delegates with time to spare.

Some visit the library to read and reminisce. The First Continental Congress used it often in 1774. The Philosophical Society is building a new home for itself down the street—a testament to this city's respect for the life of the mind. Philadelphia is hospitable to business, art, and journalism. Her 40,000 people can choose from among ten newspapers. Freedom of conscience has been guaranteed here for two hundred years. Quakers, Catholics, and Jews have their own houses of worship. And this abundance of belief is matched by an abundance of goods. The markets burst with fresh fish and vegetables, and the well-to-do can shop for luxury items shipped in from all over the world, including fine silk from China.

Philadelphia has a taste for society. There are so many parties that George Mason, one of the Virginia delegates, already has grown restless. He will write of his impatience in a letter to his son:

> *It is impossible to judge how long we shall be detained here, but from present appearance I fear until July, if not later. I begin to grow heartily tired of the etiquette and nonsense so fashionable in this city.*

But not everyone is averse to the conviviality. Many of the delegates have appetites to equal their intellects, and the taverns are busy. Rumor has it that sixty bottles of Madeira were delivered to one dinner. Sixty bottles of wine for just twelve people! Presumably any delegate present will have time to recover, or there will never be a quorum for this convention.

Friday
May 25, 1787

A<small>T LAST</small>! T<small>HE</small> federal convention has begun. Eleven days late, in the middle of a downpour, twenty-nine delegates from seven states—a quorum—finally got down to business in the State House. They accomplished just one thing today, but it was crucial: They elected a chairman. Robert Morris of Philadelphia, one of the richest men in America, made the motion:

> *Gentlemen, by the instruction and in behalf of the deputation of Pennsylvania, I have the honor to propose George Washington, Esquire, late Commander in Chief, for president of the convention.*

Washington will make only one formal speech here, but the delegates don't need his wisdom as much as his presence. The General is the most admired man in America. He is the symbol of everything this new nation wants to be: virtuous, respected, honorable, and successful. Put anyone else in that chair and the convention would lose much of its luster, much of its legitimacy.

Ironically, General Washington didn't really want to come to Philadelphia. He has served his country many years, on and off the battlefield. Now he yearns to be home at Mount Vernon, nursing his rheumatism and enjoying the life of a country squire. But the alarm of America's leading citizens summoned him from Virginia, their alarm and their letters urging him to bestow his authority on this convention personally. One came from the governor of his own state, Edmund Randolph:

I must call upon your friendship to excuse me for again mentioning the convention at Philadelphia. I feel like an intruder when I again hint a wish that you would join the delegation. But every day brings forth some new crisis and the Confederation is, I fear, the last anchor of our hope.

No one who loves his country or his image of virtue could be deaf to such a petition. The General is no marble saint. He loves fox-hunting, fancy clothes, and dinner parties. He may be the best dancer in the country. And when he loses his temper he can make the rivers run backwards. But like most educated men of this day, he believes he can mold his character by force of will—and the General's will can be as sure as cold steel. It would be surprising if he didn't remind himself of how the Roman statesmen won fame by serving their country first. The General's fame and honor are now on the line here at this convention. So is the fate of this young nation.

Monday
May 28, 1787

Benjamin Franklin made a grand entrance to the convention today. He arrived swaying in a sedan chair carried on poles by four husky convicts from the Walnut Street Jail. It's a dramatic vehicle, the first one ever seen in America, and Dr. Franklin uses it to cushion his body. It keeps the cobbled streets from stirring up his gout. But the shrewd old politician knows the value of commanding some public attention as well.

Franklin's entrance wasn't the only drama today. Pierce Butler, one of the wealthy South Carolina delegates, moved to keep the proceedings here entirely secret. When it comes to a vote, the others will agree, and they will stick to their decision with religious fervor. Nothing—not a single fact—will leak by accident from the hall all summer. George Mason wrote to his son in Virginia about the importance of the secrecy rule:

> *It is expected that our doors will be shut, and communications on the business of the Convention be forbidden during its sitting. This I think myself a proper precaution*

*to prevent mistakes and misrepresentation until the busi-
ness shall have been completed, when the whole may have
a very different complexion from that in which the several
crude and indigested parts might appear if submitted to
the public eye.*

This means the delegates will have all the freedom they
need to argue and negotiate. They can change their minds
without having to justify their every move, or launch a trial
balloon without causing an uproar back home. Naturally, the
press doesn't like the secrecy rule. A New York editor complains of "an appearance of mystery." Several newspapers
will announce scoops straight from the convention, but they
all turn out to be false. It is a summer of inventive journalism.

Others are upset as well. Thomas Jefferson, who is on a
diplomatic mission in Paris, will bridle when he hears of the
secrecy plan from his friend James Madison.

*I am sorry they began their deliberations by so abominable
a precedent as that of tying up the tongues of their members. Nothing can justify this example but the innocence
of their intentions, and ignorance of the value of public
discussions.*

Still, there will be no great public outcry against the rule
of secrecy. The people appear willing to wait and pass judgment on the results of this convention, not its procedures.
Until it ends everyone will have to be content with speculation, rumors, and gossip—and the contemplation of Dr.
Franklin's wonderful sedan chair.

Tuesday
May 29, 1787

IT'S CLEAR NOW what James Madison has been scribbling all this time in his boarding-house room. It's clear what the Virginians have been plotting during those three-hour caucuses every day before this convention even opened. Today the Virginians announced their intentions. They want to scrap the Articles of Confederation under which the United States is presently governed, and replace it with a whole new system of government. They didn't say so in those words—but that was the import of what they did say. And the other delegates realized it.

The plan—already being called the Virginia Plan—was announced in a three-hour speech delivered by that state's popular governor, Edmund Randolph. But its chief architect is James Madison. Maybe he should have delivered what he had worked so hard to prepare. But Madison is a small man with a soft and sweet voice. A scheme so revolutionary—so controversial—requires trumpet, not flute.

Edmund Randolph can sound like an entire symphony. He's six feet tall and thirty-three years old. He wears his flowing brown hair unpowdered, and his voice has been described as "most harmonious." He spoke today of great and grave consequences if this convention fails.

> *We face a most difficult crisis and we must prevent the fulfillment of the prophecies of the American downfall. . . . Look at the public countenance from New Hampshire to Georgia. Are we not on the eve of war, which is only prevented by the hopes from this convention?*

One by one Randolph laid out the fifteen resolutions of the Virginia Plan. He called for a strong national legislature that can override the states. A national executive with veto power. A national judiciary. Again and again the word echoed in their ears: national. National. National. Practically every delegate here knows the Articles of Confederation must be overhauled. It's obvious they're not working. But this proposal is sweeping. Right now the states are sovereign. They coin their own money and impose their own taxes. Nine states even float their own navies. Power rests with the state legislatures. And the national Congress—the Confederation Congress—is their servant and agent. It cannot govern the nation.

The Virginians have lost no time in bringing this convention to the heart of the matter. Without an effective and energetic government—a national government—they say this nation cannot be saved. But will the states agree?

Wednesday
May 30, 1787

EDMUND RANDOLPH TOOK the floor again today to reveal more of the Virginia Plan for an entirely new form of government. This time Randolph spelled out the scheme more precisely:

> *A Union of the states merely federal will not accomplish the objects proposed by the Articles of Confederation. A national government ought to be established consisting of a supreme Legislative, Executive and Judiciary.*

The terms "national" and "federal" are poles apart, two distinct and competing ideas. In the *federal* form of government, established six years ago under the Articles of Confederation, the thirteen states are bound together only by a loose agreement. The individual states have supreme power. They alone can enact laws over their citizens. Under a *national* government, on the other hand, Congress would have ultimate authority to impose its laws directly on the people as "citizens of the United States." That possibility terrifies some of these men, whose loyalties are to their states first and to the United States second. They fear a national government could swallow the states. Today Gouverneur Morris of Pennsylvania tried to put things in perspective:

One supreme government is better calculated to prevent wars, or render them less expensive or bloody. We had better take a supreme government now than a despot twenty years hence—for come he must.

Morris, who is emerging as one of the most vocal proponents of a strong national government, is a colorful man. At thirty-five he's made a name for himself as a lawyer and financier. He speaks eloquently, and often punctuates his sentences by thumping his wooden leg on the floor. How he lost that leg is a matter of legend. One says that Morris had to leap from a second-floor window to escape an irate husband. Gouverneur Morris seems to revel in the tale, but the truth is less romantic. He lost the leg in a carriage accident.

Morris's open reputation as a ladies' man and his liberal use of profanity have not endeared him to some of the other delegates, especially the straitlaced Yankees from New England. To them, Morris is a ''man of pleasure''—and that's meant as no compliment. But this strapping fellow is also a brilliant thinker. It is Morris who says, ''This generation will die away and give place to a race of Americans.'' The convention will determine if Gouverneur Morris is not only a man of pleasure, but a prophet, too.

Thursday
May 31, 1787

Sometimes a citizen of the modern world needs a vivid imagination to grasp the eighteenth-century notions of this federal convention. Take this idea of democracy. The debate at the State House today concerned whether the people themselves should elect any of their representatives to Congress. And some of the delegates talked about democracy as if it were a villain greater than King George and Benedict Arnold together. Elbridge Gerry of Massachusetts put it this way:

> *The evils we experience flow from the excess of democracy. The people do not lack virtue; but are the dupes of pretended patriots.*

Gerry is a New Englander who was born poor and pulled himself up by his bootstraps. So is Roger Sherman of Connecticut, yet even Sherman is dubious about democracy:

> *The people should have as little to do as may be about the government. They lack information and are constantly liable to be misled.*

Sherman began his career as a shoemaker and crowned it by helping Thomas Jefferson draft the Declaration of Independence. You'd think he and Gerry would support government by the people. But they fear the "danger of the levelling spirit." They don't believe the mass of ordinary citizens, without education and experience, could rule wisely. They want Congress to be composed of responsible men of reputation and property. So their solution is to let the state legislatures pick the House of Representatives.

On the other side are James Madison, James Wilson, and Benjamin Franklin, who believe the people will have more confidence in a Congress they have helped to choose. And that renegade aristocrat from Virginia, George Mason, who wrote most of his state's famous Declaration of Rights, spoke today for the common man:

The lower house is to be the grand depository of the democratic principle of the government. It ought to know and sympathise with every part of the community. We ought to attend to the rights of every class of the people.

Mason's argument prevailed. The majority voted for election of the lower house by the people. But even when these champions of democracy speak of "the people" they mean only certain white males. Mason himself is a man of vast holdings in Virginia—slaves included. Paradoxically, he thinks slavery is inhuman. His heart is in the right place but he is bound by the circumstances of his day. Democracy in 1787 is an idea whose time is coming, but slowly.

Friday
June 1, 1787

THERE WAS SILENCE in the hall. The delegates had just heard a proposal from James Wilson of Pennsylvania that the executive power in the new government should be placed in a single person—one man. It must have been hard for them not to turn and look at General Washington when the proposal was made. Almost everyone agrees that if there is to be one chief of state, he will be the man. No delegate wanted to appear to be slighting the General by arguing against a single executive. So no one spoke for a while.

It took prompting from Benjamin Franklin—so beloved he's above suspicion of ill motives—before others would speak their minds. Finally, Governor Edmund Randolph from Virginia was bold enough to sound a warning:

A single executive is the fetus of monarchy! I cannot see why the great requisites for the Executive department, vigor, dispatch and responsibility, could not be found in three men as well as one man.

Randolph's proposal for a three-man executive wasn't even

the most radical idea heard here. George Mason of Virginia wants three men *and* a council of advisers. Like many men in this room he's afraid of placing power in one pair of hands, especially hands that might like the feel of a kingly crown. The question proved too much to settle in one day. The delegates decided to postpone the matter for the time being. But James Wilson will continue to press his point. Wouldn't three men in the same office always be struggling for power?

Among three equal members I foresee nothing but uncontrolled, continued, and violent animosities which would not only interrupt the public administration, but diffuse their poison through the other branches of government, through the states, and at length through the people at large.

After today's session George Mason wrote a letter to his son in Virginia acknowledging that their debates weigh heavily on these men because so much is at stake:

The revolt from Great Britain and the formations of our new governments at the time, were nothing compared to the great business now before us. To view, through the calm sedate medium of reason, the influence which the establishment now proposed may have upon the happiness or misery of millions yet unborn is an object of such magnitude as absorbs the operations of human understanding.

There's no avoiding the thought. It is becoming obvious to these men that they are here not merely to tinker with the present machinery of government. They are on a task profound and enduring. James Madison says it may "decide forever the fate of republican government."

Monday
June 4, 1787

T HE UNITED STATES Government will have a *single* chief
executive, a President. That issue was finally decided after
three days of tense debate. But how much should the President be paid? It's a dilemma. Pay your public servants too
much and you invite the greedy. Pay them too little and they'll
be tempted by corruption. During Saturday's session, the
convention's resident philosopher, Benjamin Franklin, presented his argument that the executive should serve without
any salary at all. The eighty-one-year-old Dr. Franklin put
his thoughts in a letter because he doesn't quite trust his
memory anymore. And because he is growing frail, he had
another Pennsylvanian, James Wilson, read the letter aloud:

> *Sir, there are two passions which have a powerful influ-
> ence on the affairs of men. These are ambition and ava-
> rice, the love of power and the love of money. Separately
> each of these has great force in prompting men to action;
> but when united in view of the same object, they have in
> many minds the most violent effects. And of what kind are
> the men that will strive for this profitable preeminence? It*

will not be the wise and moderate, the lovers of peace and good order. It will be the bold and the violent, the men of strong passions and indefatigable activity in their selfish pursuits. These will thrust themselves into your Government and be your rulers.

Dr. Franklin conceded that he may sound utopian, but he really believes great men will put public service before private profit. As evidence, Franklin pointed to various offices in England and France that offer little or no salary. He cited the Quakers of Philadelphia who serve on committees solely out of a sense of duty. And, right in their own midst, there is General George Washington.

Have we not seen the great and most important of our offices, that of General of our armies, executed for eight years without the smallest salary, by a patriot whom I will not now offend by any other praise? I think we shall never be without a sufficient number of wise and good men to undertake and execute well and faithfully the office in question.

Out of deep respect for Franklin, the other delegates listened politely to his proposal for an unsalaried President, and then put the plan aside. They know Washington is one of a kind. Other politicians will expect to be paid. And after all, who wants a government in which only the very rich can afford to serve?

Tuesday
June 5, 1787

A WORD ABOUT Benjamin Franklin. The old man is the sage of this convention, as witty as he is wise. Legend holds that back in 1776, when he was a member of the committee to draft the Declaration of Independence, he was not allowed to write the document for fear he might conceal a joke in it. His humor came in handy during a tense debate today. The delegates were arguing over who should choose the nation's highest judges: the President, or the Congress? Dr. Franklin suggested the method used in Scotland:

> There the nomination proceeds from the lawyers, who always select the ablest of the profession in order to get rid of him, and share his practice among themselves.

Half the delegates here are lawyers. It's not recorded if any of them laughed. It seems everybody's heard of Franklin, and this convention somehow wouldn't be complete without his presence. He is celebrated on two continents as publisher, author, philosopher, politician, diplomat, and inventor, and, of course, as the man who snatched the thunderbolt from heaven. He's become a symbol of American know-how, a symbol of American genius. Here in Philadelphia his fingerprints are on dozens of projects to improve the public welfare. He helped found a hospital, a library, and a university, and to get street lights put up and garbage collected. And he's famous the world over for his pithy words of advice on almost any topic. You should, he says, go to bed early and save your money. But for young men Franklin has some other counsel. Take an old mistress, suggests the Doctor, because she'll be so grateful.

Franklin is even willing to tinker with his own inner workings. You'll find the story in his autobiography.

It was about this time I conceived the bold and arduous project of arriving at moral perfection. I wished to live without committing any fault at any time.

But he confessed his sticking point was humility. He soon found it was easier to appear humble than to be so.

Franklin is eighty-one now, troubled with gout, growing forgetful, talking a little too much. Rumor has it that a trusty companion dines out with him to make sure he doesn't spill any convention secrets. But just yesterday a friend wrote that the Doctor "exhibits daily a spectacle of transcendent benevolence by attending the Convention punctually." No one else would get such a rave review just for showing up.

Wednesday
June 6, 1787

T EN DAYS THEY have labored. Ten days. And so far not one major issue has been settled, at least not permanently. The delegates now suspect they're likely to be here in Philadelphia for a long time. Edmund Randolph said as much today in a letter home to Virginia:

> The prospect of a very long sojournment here has determined me to bring up my family . . . The plan will not be settled in its principles for perhaps some weeks hence.

No one should be surprised by this. The convention did, after all, adopt a rule that allows the same issue to be brought up for debate again and again, even after it's been voted on. For example, six days ago the delegates agreed that one house of Congress should be elected directly by the people. Today that question was raised again. Charles Pinckney of South Carolina argued, again, that the state legislatures should choose the members of the House of Representatives. Pinckney believes that the people are not "fit judges." And listen

I wish the Senate to consist of the most distinguished char-
acters, distinguished for their rank in life and their weight
of property, and bearing as strong a likeness to the British
House of Lords as possible.

That's not a peculiar notion here. All of these men are familiar with the structure of the British Parliament. There the House of Commons stands for the people and the House of Lords for the aristocracy, and they supposedly check one another's excesses. George Washington explains the idea with a homely analogy: Just as you pour your coffee into a saucer to cool it, so you cool overheated legislation by pouring *it* into a senatorial saucer.

James Wilson of Pennsylvania was one of the few dissident voices today. He argued vigorously for establishing a new American system: Let the people elect members of both houses:

The British government cannot be our model. We have no
materials for a similar one. Our manners, our laws, the
whole genius of the people are opposed to it.

Wilson argued in vain. It's liberty, not democracy, these men admire. To many of them, pure democracy is dangerous. For the safety of property and maintenance of order, they want the Senate at least once removed from the passions of the multitudes. So today they decided senators will be chosen by the state legislatures, not by the people directly. That settles it. No one has to worry about too much democracy in the Senate.

Friday/Saturday
June 8/9, 1787

A LOCAL NEWSPAPER is reporting a sensational rumor: The convention has decided to throw Rhode Island out of the Union. It's not true, but the rumor suggests how much the delegates resent the state sometimes referred to as "Rogue Island." They're unhappy that Rhode Island did not send any representatives to the convention; her leaders want no part of this attempt to form a national government. George Washington usually has a way *without* words, but Rhode Island's insolence infuriates even him:

> *Rhode Island still perseveres in that impolitic, unjust, and scandalous conduct which seems to have marked all her public councils of late. Consequently, no representation is yet here from thence.*

Even if Rhode Island were here, she would likely bristle like a porcupine at these proceedings. That's her unruly way, and has been from the start. Other states were established with an official religion. Not Rhode Island. Rhode Island was chartered under the radical principle that Church and

State should be separate. It quickly became a haven for the contrary conscience, a welcoming host to Baptists, Quakers, and the first synagogue in America.

It's not just this free thinking that grates on Rhode Island's neighbors; there's also the free spending. The state legislature is in the hands of farmers who were left deeply in debt by the revolution. To pay their debts, they printed cheap paper money to take the place of hard coin, and forced creditors to accept it as payment. They've also repudiated their debt to the federal government. Even Rhode Island's own businessmen are embarrassed by all this. They've written George Washington a letter, apologizing for the state's behavior and its absence from the convention:

The Merchants, Tradesmen, and others of this place, deeply affected with the evils of the present unhappy times, have thought proper to Communicate in writing their approbation of your Meeting. It is the general Opinion here that full power for the Regulation of the Commerce of the United States ought to be vested in the National Council.

The merchants know a strong national government would help protect their commercial interests, but they're outvoted by the farmers. If you seek a symbol of what bedevils the delegates here, reminding them of how fragile are the hopes for turning thirteen sovereign states into a united republic, it is the absence of the tiny state that has already said no.

Monday
June 11, 1787

Big states, small states: How should they be represented in Congress? Should every state be equal, regardless of size? Or should the states with more people have more representatives? The delegates tried to put this debate off as long as they could. They know it could tear the convention apart. Right now, each state, big and small, has one vote in the Confederation Congress; but in a new Congress the Virginia Plan would give the large states greater power. To the small states, this is a death sentence. Here's Gunning Bedford of little Delaware:

> *Will not these large states crush the small ones whenever they stand in the way of their ambitions or interested views? It seems as if Pennsylvania and Virginia wish to provide a system in which they will have an enormous and monstrous influence.*

And Judge David Brearley of New Jersey:

The large states, Massachusetts, Pennsylvania, and Virginia, will carry everything before them. Virginia with her sixteen votes will be a solid column indeed, while Georgia with her solitary vote and the other little states will be obliged to throw themselves constantly into the scale of some large one in order to have any weight at all.

Brearley conceded it wasn't fair to give a small state equal weight with a large one. So he made a novel proposal: Spread out the map of the United States, erase all the existing boundaries, and then divide the whole into thirteen equal parts. Equality by geography! It didn't wash.

But the small-state men continued to press their point. Look at the instructions our state gave us, they said. We are not here to annihilate the sovereignty of our states in an effort to form one nation! William Paterson, another New Jerseyan, was defiant:

I declare that I will never consent. Myself or my state will never submit to tyranny or despotism!

But James Wilson responded that little New Jersey should not have the same strength in Congress as his own state of Pennsylvania:

It is unjust. I will never confederate on this plan. If no state will part with any of its sovereignty, it is in vain to talk of a national government.

Wilson and the large states won today. The idea of proportional representation for both the House and the Senate was approved, by a very narrow margin. No doubt the issue will come up again. Thirteen states of unequal size must somehow decide how to share power in a new government, or this convention and this nation will surely end in failure.

Tuesday
June 12, 1787

Is this the very room that eleven years ago echoed with
the ringing sentiments of the Declaration of Independence?
For a spell today the talk here sounded more like that of
clerks in a counting house. The delegates were debating
numbers. How many years should a representative serve in
Congress? What about a senator? How much should representatives earn?

But these men are learned and disputatious. It was inevitable that they would argue over numbers as well as principles. The New Englanders proposed a term of only one year
for representatives. They are accustomed to annual town
meetings where local officials must answer to their neighbors. Elbridge Gerry of Massachusetts said people in New
England look on elections every year as "their only defense
against tyranny," and will never give them up. That brought
James Madison to his feet:

> *If the opinions of the people were to be our guide, it would
> be difficult to say what course we ought to take. No mem-
> ber of the Convention could say what the opinions of his*

constituents were at this time. We ought to consider what is right and necessary in itself for the attainment of a proper Government.

Madison thought representatives should serve three years. That would give them time to learn about the interests of the other states. And he thought seven years acceptable for senators. Insulated within the safety of a long term they should be able to check the passions of a lower house elected directly by the people. A term of seven years was also championed by another Virginian, Edmund Randolph:

A firmness and independence may be the more necessary also in this branch, as it ought to guard the Constitution against encroachments of the Executive who will be apt to form combinations with the demagogues of the popular branch.

But seven years struck Roger Sherman of Connecticut as too long. If senators do their duty well, he said, they will be reelected. But if they act amiss, an earlier opportunity should be allowed for getting rid of them. But when the delegates voted, the longer terms won out—three years for representatives, seven years for senators.

Benjamin Franklin then inspired about the only unanimous vote of this long day's debate. A resolution was introduced calling for the liberal compensation of congressmen. Always looking to save a penny, old Franklin moved to change "liberal" compensation to "moderate." His motion passed. Congress would get a lesson in thrift—perhaps.

Wednesday
June 13, 1787

IF THIS CONVENTION ended today, what would the new government look like? After more than two weeks of debate the delegates have agreed on a few major points—at least tentatively.

The convention has approved the idea of a national legislature with two houses. The lower house would be elected by the people, the upper by the state legislatures. In both houses, states would be represented according to their population or wealth. A single chief executive would serve a seven-year term. Most important, the national government would be supreme, with enough power to veto some state laws. But the delegates are free to change their minds at any time. So everything they've decided so far could be taken apart and put back together in an entirely different form.

No one but the delegates is aware of any of this. The secrecy rule binding the convention has worked without a hitch. But there very nearly was a breach of security the other day. One of the men lost his notes of the proceedings. Another delegate found them lying on the floor and returned them to the convention's president, George Washington. The General proceeded to scold the convention as if it were a classroom of naughty children:

> *Gentlemen, I am sorry to find that some one Member of this Body has been so neglectful of the secrets of the Convention as to drop a copy of their proceedings. I must entreat Gentlemen to be more careful, lest our transactions get into the Newspapers and disturb the public repose by premature speculations.*

The General threw the notes onto a table and said, "Let him who owns it take it." Then he walked out. No one moved. To this day the guilty party remains anonymous.

All this secrecy has bred some suspicion toward the convention. Today a Massachusetts newspaper actually begged its readers to be patient and to have faith in these Philadelphia proceedings:

> *Ye men of America, banish from your bosoms those demons, suspicion and distrust. Be assured, the men whom ye have delegated to work out your national salvation are men in whom ye may confide—their extensive knowledge, known abilities, and approved patriotism warrant it.*

The coming weeks will determine whether that faith is justified. So far the delegates have managed to shape an outline for a new government. But it is still only an outline. Many opinions and divisions remain to be reconciled before anyone can begin to hope for "national salvation."

Thursday
June 14, 1787

As soon as the delegates arrived at the State House this morning, they agreed to adjourn, and no doubt some of them headed straight for the Delaware River in search of a cool breeze. But others had work to do. William Paterson of New Jersey proposed the day off. He wants time for delegates from small states to prepare a response to the Virginia Plan.

The feelings on this and other issues are already running deep, and the passions are sure to test the rules of this convention in the days ahead. It's now becoming clear why one of the delegate's first acts back in May was the establishment of a long list of parliamentary rules to govern their proceedings here:

Every member, rising to speak, shall address the President; and whilst he shall be speaking, none shall pass between them, or hold discourse or read a book, pamphlet, or paper, printed or manuscript . . .

A member shall not speak oftener than twice, without special leave, upon the same question . . .

A member may be allowed to explain his conduct or expressions supposed to be reprehensible.

When the House shall adjourn, every member shall stand in his place, until the President pass him.

The list goes on. The rules are precise, the protocol exact. These delegates are not strangers to debate or politics. More than half have studied law. Every one of them has held a local or national office. They know the value of paying attention to debate, of not reading, yawning, or dozing when colleagues are speaking. But they're also men of the age, men of the Enlightenment. They respect reason and order and deplore excess.

Extremism in the debate of ideas is no virtue here. They believe government rests on a delicate balance of interests, on compromise. Simple courtesy and a respect for the rules are necessary to a productive meeting, and assure that each delegate is treated fairly. Finally, these men are trying to bring order to a rambunctious new country. They cannot hope that militant farmers will come to their senses, or fishing disputes between the states to a truce, if the virtues of fair play are not practiced on high. It's a lesson they take from history. Those who would govern others should first master themselves.

Friday/Saturday
June 15/16, 1787

T HERE WAS REBELLION in the State House—an open challenge to the whole idea of the Virginia Plan. The small states are alarmed. They fear being swallowed up or run over by their bigger neighbors, Virginia, Massachusetts, and Pennsylvania. So the small states have come up with their own scheme, the New Jersey Plan. It provides for a Congress with only one house and gives every state, regardless of size, an equal vote. New Jersey's William Paterson presented the plan:

> *I came here not to speak my own sentiments, but the sentiments of those who sent me. If the sovereignty of the states is to be maintained, the Representatives must be drawn immediately from the states, not from the people. And we have no power to vary the idea of equal sovereignty.*

The small states insist on equality in Congress. They think tiny Delaware, with 37,000 citizens, should be just as well represented as Pennsylvania with 360,000. But the larger states are equally adamant for proportional representation: the greater the population, the more representatives in Congress. So Paterson tried a new tack. He shifted the arguments against the large states from principle to pocketbook.

The Virginia Plan would have 270 members of Congress, coming once at least a year from the most distant parts as well as the most central parts of the republic. In the present deranged state of our finances, can so expensive a system be seriously thought of?

And John Lansing of New York tried yet another counter-argument. He said the convention was exceeding its authority even to consider establishing a supreme new government.

New York would never have concurred in sending deputies to the convention, if she had supposed the deliberations were to turn on a consolidation of the states, and a national government.

After Friday's bitter debate, Delaware's John Dickinson had a private warning for his friend James Madison: Don't trifle with the small states.

You see the consequence of pushing things too far. Some of the small States are friends to a good National Government. But we would sooner submit to a foreign power than submit to be deprived of an equality of suffrage and thereby be thrown under the domination of the large States.

The lines have been drawn. And the tensions are sharp and serious. The small states are now hinting that if they don't get their equal vote in the new government, there may be no union.

Monday
June 18, 1787

For six hours today Alexander Hamilton held this convention spellbound. He said the Union is dissolving and only a strong central government can save it. That's not news here—but Hamilton's sweeping definition of national supremacy was. He wants to base America's new government on nothing less than the British Constitution. He even called the British House of Lords "a most noble institution" because its men of property can resist popular demagogues. The key to Hamilton's thinking is that no single class or faction should have a monopoly on power:

> Give all power to the many, they will oppress the few. Give all power to the few, they will oppress the many. Both, therefore, ought to have power, that each may defend itself.

So he proposed a government with a legislature elected by the people for three years, a senate to serve for life or good behavior, and an executive chosen for life. That last hint of monarchy was audacious enough, but Hamilton went even further. He said the national government should have an absolute veto over state legislatures:

All laws of the particular states contrary to the Constitution or laws of the United States shall be utterly void.

That was too much. Hamilton's eloquence was praised by everyone, his ideas supported by none.

Hamilton is an outsider in his own New York delegation. The other two members were appointed because they agree with their governor in his opposition to this convention and to a strong central government. But Hamilton is an outsider in other ways too; he's an American without roots. He was born in the West Indies, and it's said he was illegitimate. His mother died when he was thirteen; he came to this country four years later, alone. Although he was poor as a church mouse, he married into a wealthy family. But his success is due less to nuptial connivance than to sheer brain power and ambition.

For seven years Hamilton has lobbied for a constitutional convention to give this country a government worthy of his vision for it and to make it a power in the world equal to Europe. Now that the convention is here, ironically his influence is nil. Hamilton is a man of strong convictions. He fought against the British in the Revolution, but when the war ended he helped Tories go to court to recover their property. In the army Alexander Hamilton was known as "the little lion." Today he roared mightily and was silently ignored.

Tuesday
June 19, 1787

Today the convention belonged to James Madison. He took the floor to attack the New Jersey Plan piece by piece. The plan would give Congress some energetic new powers and establish an executive and a judiciary for the country. But it doesn't go as far as the Virginia Plan—which Madison virtually wrote—in creating a union of the states under a strong central government. And because the New Jersey plan also gives the small states an equal vote in Congress, it's vigorously opposed by Madison and the large states.

So today Madison turned the New Jersey Plan on its head. In a long speech he called up examples of history all the way back to the kings of Persia to show the small states the flaws of their scheme. Madison asked: Will your plan prevent the states from encroaching on one another? No. Will it protect the Union against foreign invasion? No. And to the New Jersey Plan's insistence on "one state, one vote" in Congress, Madison asked them to look to the future—to the day when the nation admits new states into the Union from the west:

If they should come into the Union at all, they will come when they contain but few inhabitants. If they should be entitled to vote according to their proportions of inhabitants, all will be right and safe. Let them have an equal vote, and a more objectionable minority than ever might give law to the whole.

It was a powerful demonstration of knowledge, logic, and persuasion, and it contained a warning—if the small states don't reconsider their support of the New Jersey Plan, the convention will fall apart and take this struggling young nation with it:

Let the union of the States be dissolved and one of two consequences must happen. Either the States must remain individually independent and sovereign; or two or more Confederacies must be formed among them.

Not one nation but two or even more. And the New World would resemble the old: a host of rival neighbors plotting, intriguing, and battling. The prospect chills delegates who believe that in union lie strength and survival. When Madison finished speaking, the delegates took a straightforward vote: the New Jersey Plan or the Virginia Plan? Madison's Virginia Plan won, and the New Jersey Plan was dead. But as the delegates adjourned it was apparent the small states intend its resurrection in one form or another. They have retreated, not surrendered, and they will fight another day.

Wednesday
June 20, 1787

I**T'S HOT IN** Philadelphia and getting hotter, especially in
this room where the federal convention meets every day.
Some of the delegates are corpulent men. And they sweat.
This doesn't make it any more pleasant inside the State
House. The doors are closed to keep the proceedings secret.
And the windows are closed to keep out Philadelphia's no-
torious stinging flies. But not even the freshest breeze could
cool these tempers. The convention is just like the current
heat wave. It goes on and on, with no relief.

Yesterday a breakthrough finally seemed at hand. After
three weeks of debate, first on the Virginia Plan for a strong
new central government, then on the alternative proposed by
New Jersey, the delegates voted to support the Virginia Plan.
But none of this debate was for keeps. The delegates have
been meeting as a "Committee of the Whole," a parliamentary device that allows for informal discussion binding on no
one. This morning the convention went back into formal
session. George Washington, who had been sitting out with
the delegates, returned to his place at the head table as president of the convention.

The first to speak was Oliver Ellsworth, a shrewd country lawyer from Connecticut. He noted that many of the delegates were still unhappy about the strong national government called for in the Virginia Plan. And he had a shrewd country lawyer's solution:

I propose, and therefore move, to expunge the word "national."

Just drop the word. Don't call it the "national government," but "the government of the United States." A small change, but it was meant to appease the forces that don't want a central government ruled by the big states. It didn't entirely work. John Lansing of New York said that whatever it's called, the convention had no business creating a new form of government. But that was quite enough for George Mason of Virginia. Hadn't they just spent three weeks resolving this very issue?

I did not expect this point would have to be re-agitated.

But it seems everything that has come before is being re-agitated. Luther Martin, an enemy of the Virginia Plan and a man not noted for brevity, rose to speak:

I know that government must be supported; and if the one is incompatible with the other, I would support the state government at the expense of the union, for I consider the present system as a system of slavery.

Martin and the other delegates from the small states don't have the numbers to win their fight. But they do have the ability to irritate, just like those pesky Philadelphia flies.

Thursday
June 21, 1787

THOMAS JEFFERSON CALLS this federal convention "an assembly of demigods." Very generous of him, especially since he isn't here on Olympus with them. In fact, some of America's most celebrated sons are missing from Philadelphia this summer. A few of the flaming patriots of revolutionary days are not here by choice. Patrick Henry, the man who proclaimed, "Give me liberty or give me death," is absent. He wanted no part in the birth of a strong central government, which he fears this convention may produce. Virginia asked him to be a delegate, but he said he "smelt a rat" and refused.

John Adams and Jefferson couldn't be here. They are in Europe, on diplomatic missions. Adams may have the toughest job an American could have in the world right now. He's Minister to Great Britain, representing the winning nation, the United States, on the home court of a very sore loser. In his letters, Adams complains that the King and royal court by turns ignore and insult him:

I am like to be as insignificant here as you can imagine. I shall be treated with all the civility that is shown to other foreign ministers but shall do nothing. I find myself at the end of my tether. No step that I can take, no language I can hold will do any good, or, indeed, much harm.

Jefferson is in more hospitable circumstances as Minister to France. He mingles happily with artists and intellectuals, and is welcomed by noblemen as well. But he's struck by the contrasts he sees in France—the elegance of the few and the wretchedness of the multitudes. Already skeptical of arbitrary power, Jefferson writes letters home describing monarchy as a government of wolves over sheep. He hopes the New World can learn from the failures of the Old:

In this country, the people are loaded with misery by kings, nobles, and priests. Preach, my dear sir, a crusade against ignorance. Let our countrymen know that the people alone can protect us against these evils, and that the tax which will be paid for this purpose, is not more than the thousandth part of what will be paid to kings, priests, and nobles, who will rise up among us if we leave the people in ignorance.

So although Jefferson isn't here, his influence is. He's written that even though America is still a child, it already is giving hopeful proofs of genius, including this assembly of patriots. But he knows that if the new republic is to flourish, more is required than wise leaders, more than an effective and just government ruling from Olympus. Not sheep but citizens keep the wolf from the door.

Friday
June 22, 1787

How much money should congressmen be paid? And who should pay them? Oliver Ellsworth of Connecticut thinks that's something each state should decide for itself:

> *The manners of different states are very different in the style of living. What would therefore be deemed a reasonable compensation in some states, in others would be very unpopular.*

But Nathaniel Gorham of Massachusetts said all congressmen should receive the same salary. He thinks Congress can be trusted to set its own pay level:

> *I wish not to refer the matter to the State Legislatures, who are always paring down salaries in such a manner as to keep out of offices men most capable. Let the National Legislature provide for their own wages from time to time.*

It was James Madison of Virginia who got to the philosophical heart of the matter. If congressmen are paid by their

58

individual states, he said, they will be dependent on those states. In the new scheme of government where Congress should try to serve the *national* interests, Madison thought this "improper." And enabling Congress to pay itself might be even worse:

> *The members of the Legislature are too much interested to ascertain their own compensation. It would be indecent to put their hands into the public purse for the sake of their own pockets.*

So Madison offered an alternative: Fix a specific salary for congressmen, write it into the Constitution, and index it to some commodity like wheat to protect it against price fluctuations. The other delegates didn't even consider it. They couldn't agree on anything about congressional pay except that it should be "adequate."

The delegates considered another question today: Should there be a minimum age for service in the lower house of Congress? George Mason of Virginia argued that congressmen should be at least twenty-five. He admitted that when he was twenty-one his own political opinions were too crude to merit national influence. But James Wilson of Pennsylvania argued against any minimum age:

> *I am against abridging the rights of election in any shape. The motion tends to damp the efforts of genius and of laudable ambition. Many instances might be mentioned of signal services rendered in high stations to the public before the age of twenty-five.*

Wilson lost the argument. The convention voted for the minimum age of twenty-five. It may be just a coincidence, but the youngest man in this hall is twenty-six. They haven't disqualified *themselves*.

Monday
June 25, 1787

Wʜᴀᴛ ᴀʀᴇ ᴡᴇ to make of Charles Pinckney? At twenty-nine, he's one of the youngest delegates here. But he's going around telling everybody he's twenty-four, which would make him *the* youngest delegate. You can't miss Charles Pinckney. If you walked into the State House, you would spot him immediately—even in the room with Washington, Franklin, and Madison. He's the one dressed in satins and silks. With lots of lace.

Charles Pinckney is a nabob from South Carolina, a dandy in spiffy clothes—wealthy, ambitious, and so cocksure that he takes upon himself without apology the moral defense of slavery. He would be preposterous if he weren't so American.

He fought the British in the Revolutionary War. His comforts he forgoes for the taxing demands of public service. And his station as one of Charleston's finest has not diminished his opinion of the common man. The other day Alexander Hamilton called on this convention to model the new government after the British Crown and Parliament. Today it was Pinckney who replied "Never!"

The people of the United States are perhaps the most singular of any we are acquainted with . . . A system must be suited to the habits and genius of the people it is to govern.

And, says Pinckney, what makes the Americans so different from the rest of the world is the spirit of equality:

Among them, there are fewer distinctions of fortune and less of rank than among the inhabitants of any other nation. Every freeman has a right to the same protection and security; and a very moderate share of property entitles them to the possession of all the honors and privileges the public can bestow.

This equality will continue, Charles Pinckney predicted. Immigrants will be drawn here from the world over, the vast unsettled lands will be cultivated, industry will grow, and "none will be excluded by birth and few by fortune from voting." What this convention must do, Pinckney said, is create a government capable of extending to its citizens all the blessings of civil and religious liberty. This, in 1787, from a young man not yet thirty—a dandy and a patriot, conceited and far-seeing, defending slavery and the common man. So confident of the future, so full of faith in his country, and so full of contradictions. An American, to be sure.

Tuesday
June 26, 1787

Every day the delegates can look out their windows and see a different America. This city that hosts them is the largest and most fashionable in the country. But just across the yard from the State House is the Philadelphia prison. Many of its inmates are there for the crime of poverty, imprisoned for failing to pay their debts. Through the barred windows they scream at passersby or plead for charity. The men trying to create a new government are noisily reminded that America in 1787 has many faces.

There are almost four million people in the country, mostly white Protestants of British descent. But one in five Americans is a slave. The population clusters between the Atlantic Ocean and the Appalachian Mountains. In the bigger cities—Philadelphia, New York, Boston, and Charleston—an American can live as comfortably as any European. Or so the Americans say. But New York, the country's second largest city, still hasn't recovered from two big fires and the British occupation during the war. Just this year a visitor described New York as poor, ruined, neglected, and silent.

Most Americans live isolated lives. Only five percent live

in anything you could even call a town. Most rural folks never see more than a few dozen people in one place, or travel more than twenty-five miles from their birthplace. They receive maybe one or two letters a year. If they ever see a newspaper, it's usually months old. They raise just enough for their own needs: a few pigs, a little corn, chickens, and children. Salt pork and bacon are staples, vegetables are rare, and people everywhere know that the best way to preserve fruits or grain is to distill them into spirits. Visiting Europeans complain that Americans are half-drunk most of the time.

The countryside is a hard world. When farmers go broke, they can be thrown in jail or sold into servitude. Many look west for relief. Out beyond the Appalachians is rich and open land, empty except for the Indians driven there from the settled areas of the East. The mountains are hard to cross, but this year 900 flatboats will carry folks down the Ohio River in search of opportunity. How to knit all these scattered and solitary Americans together under one energetic government is the main question of this convention. But these delegates have another concern, too. Even if they succeed in creating a new government, will all those Americans out there even know it exists? Or care?

Wednesday
June 27, 1787

As if a Philadelphia heat wave isn't enough, the convention was saturated today by a gust of hot air from one of its own members. The windbag in residence is Luther Martin, the attorney general of Maryland. Martin arrived at the convention just three weeks ago, but he has already earned a place as its least favorite son. His speech today was variously described as diffuse, fatiguing, and disgusting, and it covered ground already well traveled. Martin's rambling discourse came down to this: The small states are being trampled on. He argued that the convention has no authority to alter the present system of government, which gives each state one vote in Congress. And he tried to discredit the Virginia Plan, which calls for representation based on a state's population.

My opinion is that the general government ought to protect and secure the state governments. The cornerstone of a federal government is equality of votes. States may surrender this right, but if they do their liberties are lost. If I err on this point, it is the error of the head, not of the heart.

The other delegates weren't impressed by either Martin's head or his heart, just by his lungs. His speech went on for more than three hours before he finally gave in to exhaustion.

No one was surprised by his performance. Luther Martin is known as the wild man of this convention. He's rumored to have a fondness for the bottle, especially when there's brandy in it. That hasn't prevented him from achieving a reputation as a first-class lawyer. There are stories of Martin arriving late in the courtroom after one of his many binges, taking a nip from his flask, and proceeding to argue brilliantly and successfully. No one here claims Martin is a stupid man; he did graduate first in his Princeton class. They just call him insufferable. He proved it today:

> *I would not trust a government organized on the reported plan for all the slaves of Carolina or the horses and oxen of Massachusetts.*

With his speech, Luther Martin emerged as one of the leading spokesmen for the small states. But instead of persuading anyone by his arguments, he managed to alienate the large states even farther. They can tolerate the heat but not the hot air.

Thursday
June 28, 1787

Ben Franklin asked for a miracle. The debate over representation in Congress had reached a draw. As the session began this morning, the convention was deadlocked and desperate. The delegates were frustrated by stalemate, worn down by argument and heat, almost on the verge of calling it quits. Then Dr. Franklin spoke. This alone was enough to arouse curiosity, for the old man has uttered hardly a word for days. Perhaps the other delegates were expecting him to say something light or witty. Instead, Franklin made a suggestion: Why not call on God?

In the situation of this Assembly, groping as it were in the dark to find political truth, how has it happened, Sir, that we have not hitherto once thought of humbly applying to the Father of lights to illuminate our understandings?

Dr. Franklin reminded the others that the Continental Congress had called for divine help at the start of the Revolutionary War.

Our prayers, Sir, were heard, and they were graciously answered. And have we now forgotten that powerful friend? Or do we imagine that we no longer need his assistance? I have lived, Sir, a long time, and the longer I live the more convincing proofs I see of this truth: that God governs in the affairs of men. And if a sparrow cannot fall to the ground without his notice, is it probable that an empire can rise without his aid?

And then this eighty-one-year-old man took his listeners beyond the moment to consider what will happen if they fail in their mission to forge a new government:

We shall be divided by our little partial local interests. Our project will be confounded, and we ourselves shall become a reproach to future ages. And what is worse, mankind may hereafter despair of establishing governments by Human Wisdom, and leave it to chance, war and conquest.

Franklin moved that a chaplain be hired to begin each day's session with a prayer. The move was seconded. But Alexander Hamilton and others argued against it, claiming that such a measure would only reveal the dissension inside the convention and alarm the public. And Hugh Williamson of North Carolina pointed out that there was no money to pay a preacher. In the awkward silence that followed, the idea died without a vote. There would be no miracle from on high, at least not today. Still, Dr. Franklin had required these notable men to think on their fallible ways, and to measure their duty here on a larger scale—the scale of eternity. Perhaps the old man performed his own miracle.

Friday/Saturday
June 29/30, 1787

YOU OF THE large states say you never will hurt or injure the lesser states. I do not, gentlemen, trust you.

That's Gunning Bedford of Delaware. The object of his fury is the proposal of the large states that their size should give them greater power in any new government. Carry through with it, he said, and see what happens:

If you possess the power, the abuse of it could not be checked. Sooner than be ruined, there are foreign powers that will take us by the hand. If we solemnly renounce your new project, what will be the consequence? You will annihilate your federal government, and ruin must stare you in the face.

Gunning Bedford has finally dared to admit what until now has been unspoken. The small states will leave this convention if their power and influence are diminished in a new government. And if they leave the convention, they could leave the Union.

There is no agreement. The convention is deadlocked. Days of sweaty argument have not solved the great question: Should the small states be equal to the large in Congress? No, say the large states; trust us to be fair. But the small states would just as soon trust in the goodness of Julius Caesar as that of Virginia or Pennsylvania. The words flew hard today, and hit their target:

JAMES WILSON (Pennsylvania): *I make this proposal not because I belong to a large state, but in order to pull down a rotten house and lay the foundation for a new building.*

JONATHAN DAYTON (New Jersey): *The plan on the table is an amphibious monster. It will never be received by the people.*

ALEXANDER HAMILTON (New York): *Nothing could be more preposterous or absurd than to sacrifice the rights of individual men to the rights of the states.*

RUFUS KING (Massachusetts): *My mind is prepared for every event, rather than to sit down under a government founded in a vicious principle of representation.*

So there was gloom in this hall when the afternoon session ended, and there is pessimism in their quarters tonight. Both the small states and the large know someone must compromise, but neither side is willing to make the first sacrifice. Ruin stares this convention in the face—right here and now.

Monday
July 2, 1787

T HERE WAS A showdown today, with all the tension of a Shakespearean drama. The great question came to a vote this morning: Should the large states have greater representation in Congress? After the deadlock and fury of last week, the outcome seemed inevitable. The big states would ram their plan through, the small ones would walk out in anger, and the hopes for a new government would go with them. But no one reckoned on the invisible hand of caprice writing the last act.

A few delegates didn't show up. Another changed his mind. And the vote ended in a tie. Nobody won or lost and nobody walked out. The tie vote made clear what hours of stubborn argument would not: No one can dictate the terms here. The states have to compromise. Even that disputatious Harvard man, Elbridge Gerry, can see the handwriting now:

Something must be done, or we shall disappoint not only America, but the whole world. We must make concessions on both sides.

Here's how it happened. Most of the states voted as expected. But Maryland was a surprise—with one delegate missing, her vote changed. By the time Georgia cast the final vote, the states were split, five to five.

Until now, Georgia has been siding with the large states. But two of her four delegates were absent today. The third has voted with the large states all along and was sure to stand firm. This left the fourth Georgia delegate, a lawyer named Abraham Baldwin, with the decisive vote. He's been supporting the big states, too. But today he switched, and by switching he cancelled out the other Georgian's vote, leaving the final decision still deadlocked, five states to five.

Why did Baldwin do it? Was it the pull of his roots? He was born in little Connecticut, trained at Yale, and came to Georgia three years ago. Perhaps his affections linger up North. Or perhaps this former preacher knew the convention was doomed unless somebody forced it to face reality. He did just that. There sat Washington, Franklin, Madison—all helpless. It was Abraham Baldwin, a relatively unknown migrant Yankee, who gave this convention a second chance.

Tuesday
July 3, 1787

THE DELEGATES ARE finally getting a holiday. All but eleven, that is. The eleven are on a committee appointed to find some way out of the deadlock in which the convention is mired. While they search for a compromise, everyone else is taking time off for the Fourth of July holiday.

There are plenty of diversions here in Philadelphia. The delegates can spend their free time strolling through the city's famous botanical garden or along the Schuylkill River. Or they can stroll right to one of the taverns. All roads in Philadelphia seem to lead to a tavern. There are 117. The delegates favor The Indian Queen and The City Tavern. They talk over a bottle of Madeira or brandy, or enjoy a game of backgammon.

They can go to the theater. There's a lesson or two to be picked up there as well. Eight years ago the Quakers who control the state legislature outlawed all plays. So when *Richard III* came to town, it wasn't called a play at all. It was billed as a ''series of historical lectures—in five parts—on the fate of tyranny.''

George Washington spent part of the day at that quaint

Philadelphia attraction known as Peale's Museum. Its proprietor is Charles Willson Peale, the artist who in his enthusiasm for the Old Masters named his own sons Raphaelle, Titan, Rubens, and Rembrandt. The museum is a curious mix of paintings, old bones, and other strange and wondrous objects. When Peale's not painting, he's tinkering. Right now he's trying to learn taxidermy, using some pheasants that once belonged to General Washington. The General can study his pheasants, now stuffed, as he sits for Peale to paint his portrait. There is no indication, from the work in progress, whether the General thinks the pheasants are in better shape than this convention. He will admit that his mind has been on Virginia, on his beloved Mount Vernon. In a letter home he asks his foreman, "How do the pumpkin vines look? Do your turnips come up well?" And "P.S. Keep the shrubberies clean." No wonder his country esteems him so. In the midst of great affairs of state, at moments fateful and dangerous, George Washington remembers things that grow, and thinks on the harvest.

Wednesday
July 4, 1787

ELEVEN YEARS AGO this city was filled with revolutionary zeal. Fifty-six American patriots were putting their names to the Declaration of Independence here in the State House. Today Philadelphia and the rest of the nation remembered that act of defiance with a daylong birthday party. The streets were crowded with soldiers—not in combat but in celebration. Artillery, infantry, fife and drum marched through the city before thousands of people. When the parades were over, Philadelphians crowded into the taverns and continued their revelries far into the evening. This was a day for stories of the Revolution, a day for veterans to reminisce about the bloody war and victory.

The most famous of all the veterans was conspicuous in the festivities. General George Washington was out early and often. One of his first stops was at a Calvinist Church, where he heard a young law student deliver an Independence Day speech. He reminded the General and the other delegates how much the country yearns for the success of this convention.

To you, your country looks with anxious expectation, on your decisions she rests. Methinks I already see the stately fabric of a free and vigorous Government rising out of the wisdom of the Federal Convention. I behold order and contentment pervading every part of the United States.

Similar hopeful sentiments were sounded in an editorial in the *Pennsylvania Herald*:

With zeal and confidence, we expect from the Federal Convention a system of Government adequate to the security and preservation of those rights which were promulgated by the ever memorable Declaration of Independency.

But neither the editor nor the orator nor any of those patriots celebrating in the streets know that this convention is deadlocked. Its efforts to create a new government teeter on the edge of collapse. Independence Hall is as filled with gloom tonight as it was bright with the flames of revolution eleven years ago. The delegates keep this dreadful secret to themselves. Not a word escapes to dampen the spirit of the day. But one thing is plain to General Washington and the others who came here to form a new government. Unless their search for a compromise yields results when they return to work tomorrow, there might not be many more American birthdays to celebrate.

Thursday
July 5, 1787

SOMETHING'S IN THE wind. The delegates returned from holiday knowing they must compromise or fail. So they resorted today to an old trick of political debate: If you can't find the answer, change the question. The question has been: What's the best government we can make? This week it's become: What's the most acceptable government we can get? And the committee appointed on Monday already has an answer. If the small states insist on equality in Congress and the large ones demand a greater voice to represent their greater numbers, why not give both some of what they want? Why not give each state an equal vote in the Senate, and let the larger states have more votes in the House?

Not all the delegates are buying this compromise. James Madison, James Wilson, Gouverneur Morris—the men who drew up the first plan for a new government—say there can be no substitute for principle. And the principle to them is clear: The majority ought to rule. There are more people living in the large states than the small; therefore the small ought to submit to simple justice. Madison took the floor to argue for the large states:

We are driven to an unhappy dilemma. Two-thirds of the inhabitants of the Union are to please the remaining one-third by sacrificing their essential rights. When we satisfy the majority of the people in securing their rights, we have nothing to fear; in any other way, every thing. The smaller states, I hope, will at least see their true and real interest.

The small states responded that justice is more than numbers. They do not want to put themselves at the mercy of neighbors whose size could make them bullies. And they are saying that if they can't come into the new government as equals they may not come at all.

Such hints and threats have begun to have an effect. Some of the large-state delegates now say that perhaps the first of all principles is survival, the survival of the Union. Elbridge Gerry of Massachusetts said as much today, and the convention listened.

Though I assented to the Report in the Committee, I have very material objections to it. But if no compromise should take place, what will be the consequence? I foresee a secession.

The mood here is changing. The delegates are beginning to tell themselves, "If we keep worrying about justice for all, we'll end up with a government for none." It would not be the first or last time Americans discovered the virtue of compromise. If men of principle are the true heroes of humanity, as some notable delegates believe, flexible and supple men—men who trade horses and votes—are the true heroes of political conventions.

Friday
July 6, 1787

THE MEN AT this federal convention are homebodies. The delegates miss their families and the farms and towns where they live, and no one more than George Mason. There is no place he would rather be than Gunston Hall, his plantation on the Potomac in Virginia. In all of Mason's sixty-two years, this stay in Philadelphia is the longest, and farthest, he's been away from home. So what he said yesterday is all the more striking.

> *It could not be more inconvenient for any gentleman to remain absent from his private affairs than it is for me. But I would bury my bones in this city rather than expose my Country to the consequences of a dissolution of the Convention without anything being done.*

Bury my bones in Philadelphia! For a man who loves his Virginia home as much as Mason, that's quite an admission. It reveals how hard some of these men are working to prevent this convention from going under.

Mason was a member of the committee appointed to find

a way around the present deadlock. The issue is representation in Congress, and the committee has proposed a compromise: Give every state an equal vote in one house of Congress. Let the larger states have more votes in the other house. Mason thinks the compromise should be accepted, and he's growing impatient with delegates who don't like the idea:

There must be some accommodation on this point, or we shall make little further progress in this work.

The delegates pay attention to Mason. How could they not? He wrote Virginia's Declaration of Rights when some of these men were hardly dry behind the ears. It was George Mason who first wrote these words:

All men are by nature equally free and independent, and have certain inherent rights.

And it was George Mason who wrote of freedom of speech and freedom of the press and of the right to a trial by jury. Yet he's a man torn between conscience and circumstance. Like others at this convention he owns slaves. Unlike some of them, he hates the practice and says he would release them all if there were a way. He's already on record here as saying that "this new nation ought to attend to the rights of every class of the people."

George Mason longs for his Virginia home. The other delegates know that. So they listen when this white-haired man says he will suffer a grave far from home rather than quit this convention with its work undone.

Monday
July 9, 1787

MORE BAD NEWS. Two of the delegates to this convention are about to walk out and go home. Robert Yates and John Lansing, both of New York, weren't eager to be here from the start. New York is sharply divided on the issue of a strong new government, and Lansing and Yates were sent here to represent the factions opposed to it. They've been consistently outvoted on important issues, so they are going to up and leave.

To complicate matters further, the third member of the New York delegation, Alexander Hamilton, isn't here either. He represented the forces in New York that do want a strong national government. But he was isolated by Lansing and Yates and left in frustration two weeks ago. Now he is sorely missed by his allies. General Washington wrote him a letter today. Hamilton was the General's personal secretary during the Revolutionary War. They deeply admire one another and share similar views about the importance of a strong new government.

In his letter, the usually stoic General Washington didn't sound very stoic at all:

When I refer you to the state of the Councils, they are now in a worse train than ever. In a word, I almost despair of seeing a favorable issue to the proceedings and do therefore repent having had any agency in the business. The Men who oppose a strong and energetic government are, in my opinion, narrow-minded politicians, or are under the influence of local views. I am sorry you went away—I wish you were back.

Washington in despair. Washington wishing he had never come to Philadelphia. This from the Commander-in-Chief of the Continental Army during the War for Independence, the most admired man in America. Now he can't hide his grief. One of his former army comrades saw Washington the other day and reported that the look on the General's face reminded him of its expression during the terrible months they camped at Valley Forge, just down the road from Philadelphia. We can only wonder if during this impasse at the convention, the General's mind travels there—to consider the possibility that the promise of America won by the sacrifice of his men in those freezing dark days could be squandered now in the summer heat of Philadelphia.

Tuesday
July 10, 1787

Here's an exercise in the politics of this convention. Imagine yourself a delegate from Delaware, the smallest of the states represented here. Listen to the convention haggle over how many representatives each state will have in the lower house of Congress. Today's proposal: eight delegates for Massachusetts. Eight for Pennsylvania. Ten for Virginia. For your state, one. Under this system it looks as if the lower house will have members chosen on the basis of population. That means your state, Delaware, will have to stand on a single toe, while Virginia and the other big states will have two feet to plant firmly on the ground. Or on your toe.

Delaware did see this coming. She sent her delegates off to the convention with strict instructions: Never agree to anything that would change the present system of one state, one vote. And they've done their best to honor that commandment. Remember Gunning Bedford and his threat to seek a foreign alliance rather than knuckle under to the big states. And at one point George Read came up with an idea only a tiny state could love. He suggested doing away with state boundaries altogether:

Too much attachment is betrayed to the State Govern-ments. We must look beyond their continuance. The people at large are wrongly suspected of being averse to a general government.

A few of the small-state delegates even suggested that the state lines might be erased and thirteen new boundaries drawn, making each state equal. The big states scoffed at the idea.

So why isn't Delaware walking out in protest? Two reasons. There's the proposed compromise. If it passes, each state *will* have an equal vote in the Senate. Furthermore, the arguments are beginning to open minds. Some of the delegates from Delaware and the other small states realize that a strong national government could be their best protection against any big state that tries to be a bully. Delaware already knows the indignities of dependence. In the colonial days, she was attached to New York and appended to Pennsylvania. Even now she must depend on other states to give her access to ports and trade routes. If they choose to.

So Delaware has decided to be practical. She's preparing to settle for a mere toehold in the lower house—as long as equality in the Senate and a vigilant national government can keep Virginia's big feet under Virginia's own table.

Wednesday
July 11, 1787

I T'S A SUBJECT this convention would rather avoid, but can't. The subject is slavery. And today the delegates began debate on this question. When it comes to figuring representation in Congress, how should slaves be counted? Or should they be counted at all?

Right now, in 1787, there are 600,000 to 700,000 slaves in this country. One in five Americans. They live in nearly every state. North and South alike are implicated in the system. The harbors of the North are filled with Yankee ships, carrying Yankee rum, to trade for African slaves. Slaves work as farmers or craftsmen and servants in New England and the middle states. In the South they clear the swamps and cultivate the crops.

At least sixteen of the delegates to this convention own slaves. Some acknowledge it as an odious practice. Living with it troubles them, but they are not prepared to live without it. The contradiction mocks them and haunts their very steps. When Thomas Jefferson drafted the Declaration of Independence eleven years ago, he at first included slavery in that long list of grievances directed at King George III:

The King of England hath kept a market where men are bought and sold, violating the sacred rights of Life and Liberty.

But the words cut too close to home. Jefferson himself is a slave owner. In the final version of the Declaration, all references to slavery were dropped. Now the issue faces these men again. Then they simply looked the other way. They were silent. Now they will give slavery another name. One of the proposals on the table here says representation will be determined by the number of white citizens, and three-fifths of "other persons."

It appears the new Constitution of America will actually protect slavery. The question is: How long will the conscience of America tolerate it? The story is told of a soldier in the Revolutionary War, a patriot named Enos Reeves, who came upon a slave auction in North Carolina near the end of the struggle for American independence. He saw men, women, and children in chains, and he wondered, "Is this liberty? Is this the land of liberty I've been fighting for these six years?" It is, but not for those "other persons."

Thursday
July 12, 1787

Some of the speeches this week would surprise anyone hearing only parts of them. Two of the big slave-holders in South Carolina argued that slaves should be considered the equals of free men. Charles Cotesworth Pinckney:

I insist that blacks be included in the rule of representation equally with the whites.

And Pierce Butler:

The labor of a slave in South Carolina is as productive and valuable as that of a free man in Massachusetts. And consequently, an equal representation ought to be allowed for them in a Government, which was instituted principally for the protection of property.

But there's a catch. Pinckney and Butler are not saying slaves should have the same rights as free men. They aren't saying slaves should vote. They are saying slaves are valuable—valuable as property—and should be counted for the purpose of increasing a state's influence in Congress.

That's the motive. If the convention agrees to proportional representation in the new House of Representatives, then the more people a state has, the more congressmen it gets. South Carolina—like every other state here—wants all the power it can get. So it seeks to have each slave counted. That does not sit well with the delegates from the states with fewer slaves. William Paterson of New Jersey protested:

New Jersey is against it. I can regard slaves in no light but as property. They have no personal liberty, no faculty for acquiring property, but on the contrary are themselves property and entirely at the will of the Master.

Elbridge Gerry of Massachusetts has also opposed the idea.

Why should the blacks, who are property in the South, be counted any more than the horses and cattle of the North?

And Gouverneur Morris of Pennsylvania said the people of his state would revolt if they were put on an equal footing with slaves.

So the convention agreed to a compromise: Count only three-fifths of the slaves for the purpose of representation. William Davie said that's the least North Carolina would accept. Anything less and he would leave the convention. Everyone fears just that—a walkout of the Southern states. The compromise prevailed, and this is the formula: The number of white inhabitants and three-fifths of every other description. "Every other description." When it comes to recording their decision for all to see, these men still cannot bring themselves to use the word "slave."

Friday/Saturday
July 13/14, 1787

POPULATION AND POWER go together. Under the proposed new form of government being considered by this convention, the more people a state has, the more representatives in Congress.

Most of the population in 1787 is in the North. The three biggest cities are there. Philadelphia alone has more people than Georgia. The states north of Maryland are supposed to have thirty-five representatives in the new Congress and the southern states will have thirty. But all that empty space in the South will attract settlers by the thousands. Will the North then hand over power gracefully? George Mason of Virginia doesn't think so:

> *From the nature of man we may be sure that those who have power in their hands will not give it up. If the Southern States therefore should have three-quarters of the people of America within their limits, the Northern will hold fast the majority of Representatives. One-quarter will govern the three-quarters.*

And then there's the West. An empire of open land. Everyone knows this is where the American future lies. It will fill up, rumor says, with rowdy barbarians who shoot two bears each before breakfast. So some delegates are afraid of what will happen when Congress is eventually invaded by rough and uncivilized men wearing coonskin caps and muddy moccasins. Gouverneur Morris of Pennsylvania foresees the worst:

The West would not be able to furnish men equally enlightened to share in the administration of our common interests. The busy haunts of men, not the remote wilderness, is the proper school of political talents. If the Western people get the power into their hands they will ruin the Atlantic interests.

The convention has haggled all week over these issues and now agrees: Power will be shared. There will be a census taken every fifteen years and Congress will be reapportioned according to the results. Western states will be treated equally. After all, says Roger Sherman of Connecticut, "we are providing for our posterity, for our children and our grandchildren, who will as likely be citizens of new western states as the old states." It's settled. As Americans track the sun, the nation's destiny will follow.

Monday
July 16, 1787

T HIS WAS THE day of reckoning. Everybody at the convention knew it. For weeks, the big states and small states have been feuding over whether they ought to be treated as equals in Congress. Finally today came a vote on the proposed compromise: Give every state, large or small, two senators. But let population determine the number of representatives in the House. So the roll was called: for the compromise, or against?

Massachusetts?	Divided.	Maryland?	Aye.
Connecticut?	Aye.	Virginia?	No.
New Jersey?	Aye.	North Carolina?	Aye.
Pennsylvania?	No.	South Carolina?	No.
Delaware?	Aye.	Georgia?	No.

The compromise passed. In effect, the small states won. Equality in the Senate gives them the power to offset the greater numbers possessed by the large states in the House.

The large states are dejected. This is not what they wanted, not what they expected. They have the larger population by far, and fear a tyranny of the minority over them. Governor Edmund Randolph of Virginia was angry, so angry he came close to destroying this convention with a rash act. He called for an adjournment.

I wish the convention might adjourn that the large states might consider the steps proper to be taken in the present solemn crisis.

But did Randolph mean an adjournment for the day? Or for some indefinite period of time? If these men were to adjourn and go home, it's doubtful they could ever assemble again. Whatever he meant, his bluff was called by William Paterson of New Jersey, who was equally angry at this attempt to derail the compromise:

I think, with Mr. Randolph, that it is high time for the convention to adjourn, that the rule of secrecy ought to be rescinded, and that our Constituents should be consulted. I will second it with all my heart.

Randolph realized the convention itself was now at risk. He quickly said he only meant an adjournment until tomorrow. This was finally agreed to, and the delegates went out to their taverns and inns.

It was unquestionably the critical moment for the convention. The question of representation in Congress came close to destroying any chance of forming a new government. Today's great compromise means the work continues.

Tuesday
July 17, 1787

T HE WORLD AT large so far has no idea what's going on at this federal convention. From the start the delegates have kept their word. No secrets have leaked. But there is a record of what's happening—an extraordinary record, kept by an extraordinary man, James Madison of Virginia. He set out from the beginning to record these proceedings in detail:

> *I chose a seat in front with the other members on my right and left hand. In this favorable position, I noted in terms legible what was read from the chair or spoken by the members. I was not absent a single day, nor more than a casual fraction of an hour in any day, so that I could not have lost a single speech, unless a very short one.*

It's a good thing Madison took on this burden. The official secretary of the convention, Major William Jackson, is just not up to the task, although he was recommended for the job by George Washington. Major Jackson's recorded notes are as skimpy as chicken tracks.

Madison, on the other hand, is recording the entire debate,

even the remarks uncomplimentary to "Mr. M," as he calls himself in his notes. That's characteristic of James Madison. He seems as honest as he is accomplished. Only thirty-six years old, he's already served three years in Congress. More than any other man, he orchestrated the events leading to this convention. He wrote most of the Virginia Plan that is the blueprint the delegates are now debating.

Madison knows the soul and story of mankind so well that he insists that the new American system include checks and balances. "If men were angels," he will say, "no government would be necessary." Men are not angels, so this convention struggles with the challenge he poses—to give a government enough power, without giving it too much.

Temperate. Gentle. Studious. Unfailingly dutiful. It's said he is still hurting from the loss five years ago of his heart's great love. She was a pretty sixteen-year-old named Kitty Floyd. Madison was about to leave for the wedding in New York when he received her letter breaking the engagement so that she could marry a young medical student. Madison has written to his friend Thomas Jefferson about the pain, but apparently no one else. He is as discreet about his private life as he is diligent about this convention. An extraordinary man, James Madison.

Wednesday
July 18, 1787

WITH ALL THE give and take, with all the debates over one proposal or another, it's easy to forget that the remarkable thing about this convention in the first place is that it's happening at all. Remember, this nation is to be a republic. These delegates are striving to create a government chosen by the people and accountable to the people.

In 1787 that's practically unheard of. Look at Europe, the mother of America, the example these men know best. Monarchs reign across the continent—monarchs accountable to no one. America's minister to France, Thomas Jefferson, has moved among them. He will never forget them:

> *While in Europe, I often amused myself with contemplating the characters of the then reigning sovereigns. Louis XVI was a fool; the King of Spain was a fool; and of Naples the same. They passed their lives in hunting. The Queen of Portugal was an idiot by nature. And so was the King of Denmark. The King of Prussia was a mere hog in body as well as in mind. Gustavus of Sweden and Joseph of Austria were really crazy.*

Yet against the cruelty of these royal fools, the people have no recourse. Except for Great Britain, there are no legislatures to represent ordinary subjects, no popular branches of government to check the monarchs' wills. And the will of most is for more. More power, more land, more wealth, more glory. To get more, they make love or war or both. Royal marriages weave dynasties; royal wars are fought for the sake of kingly gain. At home, they wage a different kind of war against their own people. Everywhere Jefferson looks in Europe, he sees despair, suffering, and injustice. Nine-tenths of the population, he says, are poor and enslaved so that one-tenth can live in luxury.

That is the tragic experience the men at this convention want to avoid, as they try to steer a course between monarchy and anarchy. Otherwise, George Washington could crown himself emperor and marry the daughter of Marie Antoinette. That is Europe's way. Here, a handful of men meets day after day to create a republican form of government, resistant to tyranny and open to change. Their new little republic will be an exception among nations. The old world knows it, and sends a stream of visitors to America to listen, inquire, and observe. There's a new spirit of politics in the air. They come to get a whiff of it.

Thursday
July 19, 1787

AT THE CONVENTION this week, they are inventing "the President of the United States." And they're having a hard time of it. The delegates aren't sure what kind of executive they want. They do know what they don't want. They don't want another monarch like King George III, known around here as the "Royal Brute of Britain." And they don't want anyone like the governors that the states created after they declared their independence from Britain. That is the other extreme. State governors today are weaklings, dominated by the legislatures, with little more than the duties of a clerk. These delegates are searching for some middle ground, and it's not easy to find. Even James Madison—a man with a very clear vision of what the new American government ought to be—is vague about the office of President. This is what he wrote before the convention began:

> I have scarcely ventured as yet to form my own opinion either of the manner in which the executive ought to be constituted, or of the authorities in which it ought to be clothed.

So this week the delegates are trying to reach some consensus on what the office should look like. On certain questions there is general agreement:

The National Executive shall consist of a single person.

But other issues are proving much harder. Who should choose the President? This is something these men have argued about before, and they will continue to argue about it. Here's Gouverneur Morris of Pennsylvania:

The executive ought to be elected by the people at large. If the Legislature elect, it will be the work of intrigue, of cabal, and of faction. It will be like the election of a pope.

But Roger Sherman of Connecticut said letting the people choose the President is a terrible idea:

The people will never be sufficiently informed. They will generally vote for some man of their own state.

George Mason of Virginia agreed and came up with a striking analogy:

It would be as unnatural to refer the choice of chief magistrate to the people as it would to refer a trail of colors to a blind man.

Who will choose the chief executive? Two days ago, the delegates decided that the state legislatures should do it. Today, they talked about a different plan: The state legislatures would appoint electors, who will choose the President by a complex and tricky process. It's pretty clear the delegates are still groping on this one. The office of President won't be invented in a day.

Friday
July 20, 1787

WHAT IF THE President of the United States turns out to be a scoundrel? Or a thief? Or worse? Should he be impeachable? That was the question today. Gouverneur Morris of Pennsylvania said absolutely not—the President should never be removed from office. If he's bad enough, he just won't be reelected. And who would do the impeaching? Not Congress, said Charles Pinckney of South Carolina. Definitely not Congress.

> *I do not see the necessity of impeachments. I am sure they ought not to issue from the Legislature, who would hold them as a rod over the Executive, and destroy his independence.*

Just about everyone else in the debate thought otherwise. Their arguments were filled with skepticism about human behavior. And an awareness that the President will be a mere human. Just listen to their fears. This is James Madison:

He might lose his capacity after his appointment. He might pervert his administration into a scheme of peculation or oppression. He might betray his trust to foreign powers.

Fellow Virginian Edmund Randolph:

Guilt wherever found ought to be punished. The Executive will have great opportunities of abusing his power, particularly in time of war when the military force and the public money will be in his hands.

And a third Virginian, George Mason:

Shall any man be above Justice? Above all, that man who can commit the most extensive injustice?

Then Gouverneur Morris took the floor again to announce a change of heart. He had argued against impeachment, but the debate persuaded him he was wrong:

I am now sensible of the necessity of impeachments. The Magistrate is not the King. The people are the King.

Frankly, it's surprising these delegates took so long to decide that a rogue in the presidency should be thrown out. They've certainly seen their share of scoundrels and strange characters in high office. A colonial governor of New York was rumored to be a transvestite who reportedly posed for a portrait in his dress. Some of the governors feathered their nests with bribes, or sold appointments and land grants. Could the President of the United States turn out to be a crook? These men thought it over today and decided to take no chances. Impeachment will be a possibility.

Monday
July 23, 1787

I<small>F PRIZES WERE</small> being awarded to the delegates who were the slowest getting here, the award ceremony would have to be today. Eight weeks after this convention opened, New Hampshire's two delegates finally straggled in and took their seats. You might think they walked to Philadelphia. They didn't. The New Hampshire legislature was just slow and stingy. It named its delegation way back in January, but then wouldn't vote a penny's worth of travel expenses. Finally delegate John Langdon, a rich merchant, said he would pick up the tab himself.

Those two New Hampshiremen would complete the group portrait of this convention, if only the delegates would sit still long enough for one. They won't. Many of them come and go as if constitution-making is far down on their list of priorities. Gouverneur Morris, that man of many public and private affairs, took three weeks off in June to cultivate them. William Livingston is simultaneously a delegate from and the governor of New Jersey. He's been slipping back and forth across the state line on official business. Three of these men are also members of the Confederation Congress.

They're up in New York this month, doing their legislative duty.

Some delegates fear the high expenses for room and board will drive them away. Last month North Carolina's delegation wrote home for more money:

> *Though we sit from day to day, Saturdays included, it is not possible for us to determine when the business before us can be finished. For this reason we submit to your Consideration the Propriety of furnishing us with an additional Draft for two months' Service.*

Absenteeism is serious. Seventy-four delegates were named to this convention. Fifty-five have shown up at one time or another. Yet often only about thirty are on the floor at any given session. As summer drags on, the convention could simply melt away or ultimately be challenged as a minority report. What prevents its demise altogether is the presence of the faithful regulars, among others Washington, Wilson, Franklin, Randolph, and the tireless James Madison. Well, almost tireless. Last week Madison complained by mail to Thomas Jefferson:

> *I have taken lengthy notes of everything that has yet passed and mean to go on with the drudgery. I am led by sundry circumstances to guess that the work will not be very quickly dispatched.*

Inventing a new government is proving to be slow work, slower even than that long journey down from New Hampshire to the Delaware.

Tuesday
July 24, 1787

JAMES WILSON WILL fool you. Friends say he isn't really cool and aloof—that regal bearing is just his way of keeping his glasses from sliding down his nose. And he doesn't look like a radical. He was a bookkeeper in Scotland, came to this country when he was twenty-three, and is now a wealthy Philadelphia lawyer. But James Wilson is the fiercest democrat at this convention. He believes passionately that people can and should rule themselves. At the convention, he takes the floor more often than almost anyone else, arguing always for the common man:

> *I wish for vigor in the government but I wish that vigorous authority to flow immediately from the legitimate source of all authority, the people. The government ought to possess not only the force, but the mind or sense of the people at large.*

Others agree that Wilson is brilliant—the intellectual equal of John Adams and Thomas Jefferson. Naturally, when the convention appointed a committee today to begin drafting a

Constitution of the United States, Wilson was on it. He has thought to the heart of the problem: how to establish a strong central authority while preserving the rights of the states and citizens:

Why should a National Government be unpopular? Has it less dignity? Will a citizen of Delaware be degraded by becoming a Citizen of the United States?

To James Wilson the ideas of democracy and nationalism are only common sense. Literally. He brought with him from Scotland the new ideas of a school of philosophy called just that—"Common Sense." He believes that every person has an intuitive understanding of moral truth and natural law. Ideas that seem simple common sense really are. And common sense says that the purpose of human life is happiness. The aim of human society is to help all members attain happiness. And listen to this:

All men wherever placed have equal rights and are equally entitled to confidence.

When Wilson says "all," he has in mind a pretty broad company. He was just about the only man here who said the people should elect the Senate. The other delegates wanted that left to the "better sort" of men. But Wilson believes that if everyone is equally gifted with moral understanding, why shouldn't everyone be equally able to elect a senator?

You can bet that when James Wilson put his signature on the Declaration of Independence eleven years ago, the sentence "all men are created equal" was more to him than rhetoric. It was a statement of common sense.

Wednesday
July 25, 1787

THESE DELEGATES STILL are having a hard time trying to figure out how the President of the United States should be elected. Should the people decide? Should the Congress decide? They can't decide. Now there's even been a suggestion to leave the choice partially to chance.

James Wilson of Pennsylvania came up with the idea. Why not choose electors by lot from among the members of Congress and let them pick the President?

Suppose there are ninety people in the legislature. Put in ninety balls. A small number of those balls will be gilded. Those who draw the gilded balls will be the electors.

But Elbridge Gerry of Massachusetts said wait just a minute:

That is committing too much to chance. If the lot should fall on a set of unworthy men, an unworthy Executive must be saddled on the Country.

Gouverneur Morris of Pennsylvania, never shy about expressing his opinions, said the proposal for a lottery might seem far-fetched at first, but "better chance should decide than intrigue."

This agitation isn't surprising. The country has never had a President before. So while these men agree on the need for a strong chief executive, they have no experience in how to pick him. Most don't trust the people to choose a President directly. It's too easy for demagogues to whip up popular passions. And if the legislature makes the selection, should both houses decide, or just one? Won't there be such horse-trading that the President will wind up a tool of the factions that got him the job? These are difficult questions, with no easy answers. The delegates can't even agree on how many years the President should serve:

LUTHER MARTIN: *Eleven years!*
ELBRIDGE GERRY: *Fifteen years!*
RUFUS KING: *Twenty years!*
WILLIAM DAVIE: *Eight years!*

At one point Gerry threw his hands up and said, "We seem to be entirely at a loss." That was the only point they could agree upon.

And what about James Wilson's idea of the gilded lottery? No one was really satisfied with that, not even Wilson. He said he really wants to see the President elected by the people of the United States. If he's going to gamble, he'd prefer to gamble on them.

Thursday
July 26, 1787

YOU CAN UNDERSTAND why the delegates to this federal convention are tied in knots over the role of the President when you consider this fact: Every one of these men grew up the subject of a king. And every one of them wants never to be subject to a king again. You can hear that in almost all their debates on the powers of the presidency. Take this tough question: Should the President be able to run for reelection? Or would that tempt him to think he could stay in office permanently, just like a monarch? George Mason of Virginia was emphatic:

> A second election ought to be absolutely prohibited. I hold it as an essential point, as the very palladium of civil liberty, that the Executive should at fixed periods return to that mass from which he was at first taken, in order that he may feel and respect those rights and interests.

But if the President is not to be reelected, there's another danger. The most capable men might be turned out of office simply because their time is up. So James Wilson argued there should be no restriction whatsoever on how many terms the President can serve:

> *If the Executive should come into office at thirty-five years of age and his continuance should be fixed at fifteen years, at the age of fifty, in the very prime of life and with all the aid of experience, he must be cast aside like a useless hulk.*

Gouverneur Morris of Pennsylvania raised another point. If the President is ineligible for a second term, he might be tempted into corruption:

> *Ineligibility tends to destroy the great motive to good behavior, the hope of being rewarded by a reappointment. It is saying to him, "Make hay while the sun shines."*

That warning was ignored. The convention voted once again to limit the President to a single seven-year term. Under the rules the delegates could change their minds yet again before their work is finished. And they're beginning to think seriously about when that might be.

Tomorrow the special five-man committee will sit down to start writing the first draft of a new Constitution. It's not that all the details have been worked out. Far from it. But they want to put down on paper what they have so far agreed on. The committee has ten days before it reports. In the meantime, the convention will recess. This will be the first long holiday the delegates have had since they began their work in May. General Washington, for one, intends to spend some of his free time fishing for trout. That's about the only thing that can be done this summer without a committee.

Friday
July 27, 1787

No sooner had this convention adjourned for ten days than Roger Sherman climbed aboard a stagecoach bound for New England. He says he'll be back when the recess is over, and if this Connecticut Yankee says it, he means it. Still, it's a long, rough trip for such a short stay, especially for a man of sixty-six.

Roger Sherman, though, is a Puritan who hungers for duty the way some men hunger for money. And duty means discipline. He once claimed he had his emotions under control by the time he was twenty-one. He strikes some of the other delegates as, well, odd. Here's what Georgia delegate William Pierce has to say about Sherman:

He is awkward and unaccountably strange in his manner. The oddity of his address and that strange New England cant which runs through his speaking make everything that is connected with him grotesque and laughable. And yet he deserves infinite praise. No man has a better heart or a clearer head.

What a stranger wouldn't know about Roger Sherman is that he is a self-made man who started out as a shoemaker, taught himself law, and went on to hold just about every public office Connecticut has to offer—sometimes four or five of them at the same time. He was quite well-off when the troubles with England came, and he is a conservative at heart. But everything he owned he put at risk as a patriot. He helped draft the Declaration of Independence and the Articles of Confederation, and he has been one of the most diligent delegates at this federal convention. "Come now and let us reason together." That's Roger Sherman's philosophy.

People trust him. John Adams called him "honest as an angel." Thomas Jefferson said that "Roger Sherman has never said a foolish thing in his life." Quite a compliment when you consider how many years Sherman has been around. He started out in public life as a young man who knew when to talk and when to keep quiet. They still remember in Connecticut how he would tell other politicians, "When you are in a minority, talk. When you are in a majority, vote."

Here at this convention, Roger Sherman was more responsible than just about anyone for putting together the great compromise on how the states will be represented in Congress. That saved the convention from almost certain failure. There are celebrated heroes in Philadelphia this summer, and men not quite so celebrated who make committees work. It takes both to produce a nation.

Monday
July 30, 1787

WHAT IS AN American anyway? And what is America going to be? Cut through all the debate of this convention, and those two questions are the heart of the matter. Gouverneur Morris of Pennsylvania put things very bluntly the other day. He said there is something sorely lacking in the proposals already put before the delegates:

Among the many provisions which might have been urged, I have seen none for supporting the dignity and splendor of the American Empire.

The American Empire. Not Virginia's empire, or Maryland's. The American Empire. In other words, Morris is asking, do we think big and see a single American people? Or do we let local and petty jealousies tie us down forever? If our ambitions are great, Morris said, then we will need a supreme national government to act boldly for all. He argued that the states are but an invention of circumstance. If they ceased to exist altogether, America would remain:

What if all the Charters and Constitutions of the states were thrown into the fire and all their demagogues into the ocean? What would it be to the happiness of America?

There you have it. Are we to be the people of this state or that, or citizens of America? Earlier in the convention, James Wilson of Pennsylvania recalled the spirit of 1776:

Among the first sentiments expressed in the first Congress, one was that Virginia is no more, that Massachusetts is no more, that Pennsylvania is no more. We are now one nation of brethren. We must bury all local interests and distinctions.

Eloquent, yes. Persuasive, not yet. The politics, customs, and laws of each of the thirteen states are rooted too deeply in local affections. My country? My country is Virginia. My country is Maryland. My country is New Hampshire. Here in 1787, America fully a nation exists in the imagination only.

Tuesday
July 31, 1787

THOMAS JEFFERSON CALLS them demigods. And their press reviews are even better:

> *The grand national convention now sitting in Philadelphia is the most respectable body of men ever convened in the Western World.*

> *A wonderful display of wisdom, eloquence, and patriotism.*

> *The collective wisdom of the continent.*

No question about it. The delegates to this convention are among the foremost men of America. Two of them, George Washington and Benjamin Franklin, are celebrated the world over. Eight signed the Declaration of Independence. Twenty-one fought in the Revolutionary War. Most have served in Congress. They're lawyers, merchants, planters, financiers. Some are self-made men. Others were born wealthy.

Robert Morris of Pennsylvania is said to be the richest man in the country, and one of the most hospitable. Respectable visitors in Philadelphia are always invited for tea at his mansion just a few blocks from the State House. Right now General Washington is staying with the Morris family during the convention. It's not just that the garden reminds him of Mount Vernon. It's not just the good food on the Morris table. Washington also knows that were it not for Robert Morris he might have been hanged on a British yardarm.

In the last days of the Revolution, the United States treasury was literally empty. There was no money left to transport Washington's army from New York to Yorktown, where the British forces were gathered. But Morris, the new nation's superintendent of finance, put his great skills to work and found the money in the nick of time. Washington and his men reached Yorktown to force the surrender of the redcoats, and the war was over. General Washington doesn't forget such things.

Morris was investigated some years ago on charges of turning his public service into personal gain. He did direct business to his firm at a profit, but he was cleared of any illegal conduct. And he still takes financial risks that would chill a more timid man; he engages in bold speculation that could some day bring him down. But the whispers about Morris are drowned by the chorus of gratitude for his service to the country. Around Philadelphia people talk about "the great man." Even George Washington knows the man they mean is Robert Morris.

Wednesday
August 1, 1787

So FAR WILLIAM Blount of North Carolina has not said a word at this convention. But he's no slouch when it comes to action. One of the big questions facing these delegates is what to do about the unsettled western territory. Though he keeps it to himself, Blount has his own answer. He's buying it, tens of thousands of acres of it, and to get it he doesn't hesitate to use bribery, forgery, and fraud.

There's a paradise of opportunity out West. The vast wilderness stretching from the Appalachian Mountains to the Mississippi River is a wealth of rich soil, abundant rivers, and plentiful forests, with fish and game to spare and plenty of elbow room. This huge territory inspires dreams of wealth and ease. It also inspires greed, deceit, and sheer stupidity on a scale in keeping with its grandeur. Just about everyone wants a piece of the West, and some are so dazzled by the prospect of getting rich they invest thousands of dollars they don't even have.

Look at James Wilson, the delegate from Pennsylvania. He's over his head in speculation out West, and that's both sad and significant, given the man's intellect and his promise as a leader in the new government. But James Wilson can hardly look over his shoulder this summer without seeing a creditor in hot pursuit. Other delegates have paper fortunes, built on speculation and hope. Some are perfectly legitimate. George Washington and Benjamin Franklin are investors in land. Some are more calculated, knowing the value of western land will be increased if a strong national government builds roads and canals to the frontier and sends militia to protect its development. And some, like William Blount, are simply crass. So far as he's concerned, you can never be too rich. If the law limits how much land one person can buy, he invents a dozen people on paper, all of whom want to buy land next to his. If another law requires a land commissioner to approve a deal, Blount will cut him into the profits. This is how Blount wrote to one of these public servants:

> *In order that we may both obtain our purposes, it is necessary that our acts should tend to our mutual advantage. There's an old proverb which says, "Make hay while the sun shines." I wish you an agreeable journey and great choice and great plenty of Cheekamagga squaws.*

It's an old story in a new land. The problem of the Great American West in 1787 is the problem of every Garden of Eden. There are snakes in it.

Thursday
August 2, 1787

NOW THAT THE convention is in recess, some of the delegates have gone home for a brief visit with their families. We can only guess what they have to say to their wives about the work here. Women have no voice in this convention and will have none in the new Constitution. The prejudice of the day was expressed in a ruling by Oliver Ellsworth—a delegate to this convention—when he was a judge in Connecticut; he said a woman should not have the power to make a will because "the government is not placed in her hands" and it would only generate "endless teasing and discord."

And listen to the popular poet John Trumbull:

> *Why should girls be learned and wise?*
> *Books only serve to spoil their eyes.*
> *The studious eye but faintly twinkles.*
> *And reading paves the way to wrinkles.*

That's the prejudice. The truth is women in 1787 exhibit character and industry equal to men, and they have since colonial days. There were soldiers to fight the Revolutionary

War because the women who stayed behind kept the family farms and mills running. Just last year a widow in New Jersey named Rachel Wells petitioned Congress with this reminder:

I have done as much to carry on the war as many that now sit at the helm of the government, and with no notice taken of me. Now gentlemen, is this liberty?

And Abigail Adams of the noted Massachusetts family has this lament:

Patriotism in the female sex is the most disinterested of all virtues because we are excluded from honors and offices, deprived of a voice in legislation, obliged to submit to those laws which are imposed upon us.

Consider Eliza Lucas Pinckney of South Carolina. She took over her father's plantations near Charleston when she was seventeen. Now she's celebrated here and in Europe for her knowledge of agronomy. It was she who turned indigo into a mass-produced crop. Manager of three plantations, Eliza Pinckney is also the mother of four children. One of them, Charles Cotesworth Pinckney, is a delegate to this convention. Think about it. He can vote, she cannot. He can hold office, she cannot. He can help write the Constitution, she cannot. Eliza Pinckney gives the cause of freedom its sons, soldiers, and statesmen. But she cannot be present at the birth of a nation.

Friday
August 3, 1787

SOMEBODY FINALLY TALKED. Some delegate, it seems, has broken the convention's rule of secrecy and leaked to the press. Newspaper readers from Philadelphia to Boston have been poring over this little item:

So great is the unanimity, we hear, that prevails in the convention that it has been proposed to call the room in which they assemble Unanimity Hall.

That chamber where the delegates have been fighting and fuming and threatening for weeks—Unanimity Hall? Some leak. Unless, of course, it was planned that way, a little disinformation to soothe the public's anxiety about the progress of the convention. Would any of these illustrious delegates do such a thing? Maybe. Think about Benjamin Franklin. He's an old newspaperman himself and an artful politician. It would be just like him to combine the power of suggestion with the power of the press.

The leak was a treat for the nation's editors, who have been striving this summer to print any news about the mysterious convention. The *Independent Gazetteer* has to make do with chatty notes about the celebrities in town:

> *Notwithstanding the tempestuous weather, the amiable and illustrious General Washington proceeded to the University to hear a Lady deliver a Lecture on the Power of Eloquence.*

The *Pennsylvania Gazette* admits frankly it doesn't know what's going on:

> *We are all anxious to hear what the Federal Convention are doing, and from their silence and secrecy are hopes in something will be done of future advantage to America.*

This is pretty thin fare about so critical a public question—but the silence from the convention isn't unusual. Secrecy is standard operating procedure for the government in 1787. Newspapermen have never been allowed into the meetings of Congress. Only two state legislatures hold open meetings. A politician's duty is to be dignified, not accountable, and the press's duty is to let him. For now.

The delegates' holiday is almost over. On Monday they'll all meet again at the State House to start debating the first draft of a Constitution of the United States. And the newspapermen will all be in their shops, hoping for more leaks—something really juicy.

Monday
August 6, 1787

THESE LAST TEN days, while everyone else was on vacation, a five-man committee labored away. Their task: to take everything the convention has agreed to since May and put it into some cohesive order. Now, on this first Monday in August, there is finally a first draft of a new Constitution. It has seven large pages with wide margins on the left for delegates to make their notes and corrections. There is a preamble, with the arresting beginning "We the People," and then there are twenty-three articles.

Four of the five members of the drafting committee are lawyers. So you might expect they would come up with something full of complicated lawyerly language. But no, this is a clear and concise document. Edmund Randolph of Virginia insisted on it:

In the draft of a fundamental constitution, two things deserve attention. To insert essential principles only and to use simple and precise language.

Essential principles only. That's how you create a document that will serve not just the needs of the moment. Randolph is well aware that the United States might someday face situations these delegates could never imagine. So he thinks going beyond ''essential principles'' would only invite problems in the future:

> *The operations of government would be clogged by rendering those provisions permanent and unalterable, which ought to be accommodated to times and events.*

In other words, the Constitution is built on a certain bedrock foundation, but its specifics are not carved in stone. And what is that bedrock? The government this draft outlines is essentially what James Madison and the other Virginians proposed two and a half months ago. It is a strong national government, with three separate branches—legislative, executive, and judicial. Each has the power to check the others. None of this is final, of course. The delegates will go over this draft point by point. The final result may bear little resemblance to what is on the table. But this is still a momentous step. For the first time, we have a document—a proposed Constitution of the United States.

Tuesday
August 7, 1787

MANY WEEKS AGO this convention agreed that the House of Representatives will be elected by the people. But which people? Today Gouverneur Morris of Pennsylvania argued that only property-owners should be eligible to vote.

> *Give the votes to the people who have no property, and they will sell them to the rich, who will be able to buy them. Children do not vote. Why? Because they lack prudence, because they have no will of their own. The ignorant and the dependent can be as little trusted with the public interest.*

If that sounds harsh, just listen to John Dickinson of Delaware:

> *Freeholders are the best guardians of liberty. Restriction of the right to them is a necessary defense against the dangerous influence of those multitudes without property and without principle.*

Many of these men are simply following the example they know best—that of England. There, only property-holders vote for members of Parliament. But George Mason of Virginia suggested they're becoming too dependent on the British example:

We all view things too much through a British medium. The true idea in my opinion is that every man having evidence of attachment to and permanent common interest with the Society ought to share in all its rights and privileges. Does nothing besides property mark a permanent attachment?

Then Benjamin Franklin took the floor. The old man always argues for the common folk, and today was no exception:

It is of great consequence that we should not depress the virtue and public spirit of our common people. I do not think that the elected have any right to narrow the privileges of the electors. The sons of a substantial farmer, not being themselves freeholders, would not be pleased at being disfranchised.

Finally, the delegates voted against the idea that only property-owners should be permitted to vote. Instead, they decided to leave voting rights up to the individual states. But there's the catch. Most of the states already have some kind of property qualifications of their own. So right now, in 1787, voting will for the most part be limited to white males—white males with property.

Wednesday
August 8, 1787

GOUVERNEUR MORRIS BROKE the unwritten rule today, the unwritten rule that says: When the subject is slavery, don't make waves. Talk about numbers, talk about representation; whatever you do, don't talk about morality. But today, Gouverneur Morris did:

> *Slavery is a nefarious institution. It is the curse of heaven on the States where it prevails. Every step you take through the great regions of slaves presents a desert increasing with the increasing proportion of these wretched beings.*

Morris's speech was a surprise attack. The delegates weren't even planning to discuss slavery today. They've already agreed on the three-fifths compromise: A state is entitled to representation in the lower house based on its white population plus three-fifth of its slaves. Today they were supposed to figure out the number of representatives each state will get. But Morris saw a chance to turn the numbers issue into a moral issue, and he took it—arguing that representation should be based on the number of free citizens only. Otherwise the South gets an unfair advantage:

> *The inhabitant of Georgia and South Carolina who goes to Africa, and in defiance of the most sacred laws of humanity tears away his fellow creatures from their dearest connections and damns them to the most cruel bondages, shall have more votes in a Government instituted for the protection of the rights of mankind, than the citizen of Pennsylvania or New Jersey who views with a laudable horror, so nefarious a practice.*

No question at this convention is simple. Morris has things on his mind in addition to the evil of slavery. He's angry that the three-fifths "compromise" seems to give the South much more than it gives the North. But he's also taking a longer view than most of his fellow delegates. He's considering what the compromise will say about the United States to future generations:

> *I would sooner submit myself to a tax for paying for all the Negroes in the United States, than saddle posterity with such a Constitution.*

Gouverneur Morris is a spellbinding orator. One delegate says that when he speaks, "he charms, captivates, and leads away the senses of all who hear him." But today his oratory charmed practically no one. Slavery is nefarious, many delegates agree. It's also a fact of life for half the country. Right now morality is too divisive a luxury for these delegates, who must fashion a government both halves of the nation will accept. So when Morris broke the unwritten rule, the convention listened politely—and then ignored him.

Thursday
August 9, 1787

Should foreigners be allowed to serve in Congress? And just what is a foreigner anyway? Those were two of the questions the delegates tried to answer today. Gouverneur Morris of Pennsylvania thinks no one should be a senator who hasn't been a citizen for at least fourteen years. After all, Morris said, it takes seven years to apprentice as a shoemaker. Pierce Butler of South Carolina, who came to America as a young officer in the British Army, agreed that is a reasonable restriction:

> *Foreigners without a long residence here bring with them ideas of Government so distinct from ours that in every point of view they are dangerous. If I myself had been called into public life within a short time after coming to America, my foreign habits, opinions and attachments would have rendered me an improper agent in public affairs.*

James Madison argued against the proposal. Fourteen years is far too long, he said. Such a wait would discourage many desirable people from coming to America.

But Gouverneur Morris said the doors to the legislature should not just be thrown open:

There is a moderation in all things. It is said that some tribes of Indians carry their hospitality so far as to offer to strangers their wives and daughters. Is this a proper model for us? I would admit them to my house, I would invite them to my table, would provide for them comfortable lodgings. But I would not go so far as to bed them with my wife!

All this touched a sensitive chord in James Wilson. Pennsylvania is his home now, but he was born in Scotland and didn't arrive here until he was twenty-three:

My feelings are perhaps peculiar, since I am not a native. There is the possibility, if the ideas of some gentlemen should be pursued, that I would be incapacitated from holding a place under the very Constitution which I have shared in the trust of making.

Wilson is not so peculiar. Eight of the delegates were born outside the United States. Finally, the convention reached a compromise: nine years of citizenship to be a senator, seven years to run for the House of Representatives. So foreigners are welcome to be a part of this new government. They'll just have to be a little patient.

Friday
August 10, 1787

T HE CONVENTION CONSIDERED putting a price tag on public service today. Charles Pinckney, who comes from one of the wealthiest families in South Carolina, argued that high officials should be men of wealth:

> *I am opposed to the establishment of an undue aristocratic influence in the Constitution, but it is essential that the members of the Legislature, the Executive, and the Judges should be possessed of competent property to make them independent and respectable.*

Pinckney even proposed a figure for each office. The President, he said, should be worth one hundred thousand dollars, federal judges and members of Congress at least half that. Almost every state requires its legislators to own property. But should similar requirements be included in the Constitution of the United States? John Dickinson of Delaware is offended by the very idea:

> *I doubt the policy of interweaving into a Republican con-*

*stitution a veneration for wealth. . . . It seems improper
that any man of merit should be subjected to disabilities
in a Republic where merit is understood to form the great
title to public trust.*

James Madison of Virginia also argued against Pinckney's
idea.

*A Republic may be converted into an aristocracy or oli-
garchy by limiting the number capable of being elected.
Qualifications founded on artificial distinctions may be
devised by the stronger in order to keep out partisans of a
weaker faction.*

The issue was settled today with a few words of wisdom
from Benjamin Franklin:

*I dislike everything that tends to debase the spirit of the
common people. Some of the greatest rogues I was ever
acquainted with were the richest rogues. This Constitution
will be much read in Europe, and if it should betray a
great partiality to the rich, it will not only hurt us in the
esteem of the most liberal and enlightened men there, but
discourage the common people from removing to this
Country.*

In his daily record of the proceedings, James Madison
reports that Charles Pinckney's motion was rejected by such
a resounding ''no'' that no one even bothered to count the
votes. So an officeholder will have to be an American, a
confirmed resident, and mature—but he won't have to be
rich.

Monday
August 13, 1787

It has occurred to the men at this convention that someone must pay for the government they're creating. That means *taxes*. Bold patriots shudder at the thought. They remember the rallying cry of the Revolutionary War: "No taxation without representation." That motto shook the mighty British Empire. A touchy subject, taxes.

The question dividing the convention right now is who should levy taxes. Who in Congress will have the power of the purse? Should it be the House of Representatives alone? Its members are to be elected directly by the voters, so many delegates believe the House will be more responsive to the will of the people.

Or should the Senate also be able to propose tax bills? Some delegates think senators would do a better job because they're more experienced in business affairs. But others disagree. Senators are to be elected by the state legislatures instead of the people. The Senate is therefore viewed with deep suspicion by some of these men, who think it smells of aristocracy. George Mason of Virginia put it his way:

The Senate does not represent the people, *but the* States *in their political character. In all events I contend that the purse strings should be in the hands of the Representatives of the people.*

So today Edmund Randolph of Virginia proposed giving the House the sole right to initiate tax bills. James Wilson of Pennsylvania objected. He said the Senate must at least share control:

It is to be observed that the purse has two strings, one of which is in the hands of the House of Representatives and the other in those of the Senate. Both houses must concur in the untying.

And then Elbridge Gerry of Massachusetts objected to the objection. He warned that any attempt to remove the power of taxation from the sole control of the House—from the *people*—would turn them against the Constitution and lead to its defeat:

Taxation and representation are strongly associated in the minds of the people, and they will not agree that any but their immediate representatives shall meddle with their purses. In short, the acceptance of the plan will inevitably fail if the Senate is not restrained from originating Money bills.

The delegates couldn't reach agreement today. They'll have to try again, or the new Constitution won't be worth the paper it's printed on. For the moment, these delegates are finding taxation *with* representation every bit as thorny a problem as taxation without it.

Tuesday
August 14, 1787

THE SUBJECT TODAY was ambition, and the men at this convention know what *that* is. The question was whether to encourage ambition or restrain it. Some say the only way to get the best, most competent people to serve in Congress is to let them hold other government offices at the same time: to be both senator *and* secretary of state, for example. Charles Pinckney of South Carolina thinks that's a fine idea. Let the Senate become "a school of public ministers, a nursery of statesmen."

But other delegates have doubts. They're not sure anyone who craves power should be entrusted with it. If they permit a senator to hold two offices at once, don't they risk turning an appetite for power into an addiction? George Mason of Virginia suspects that public officials would spend their time creating influential and high-paying positions for one another just like the corrupt aristocrats of the Old World:

It would encourage that exotic corruption which might not otherwise thrive so well in the American Soil—and would

132

complete that Aristocracy which is probably in the contemplation of some among us.

Not so, said James Wilson of Pennsylvania. He insisted that putting too many restrictions on members of Congress would only drive away the most capable men, the men this country needs most:

To render its members ineligible to National offices would take away its power of attracting those talents which are necessary to give weight to the Government and render it useful to the people.

Gouverneur Morris of Pennsylvania agreed. Why do we expect that lawmakers who win elections will be corrupt, he asked. They are the very ones who have passed the test of public scrutiny.

The argument ended in a draw. No decision today. But these men will find hard to forget something said by John Francis Mercer of Maryland. He reminded them that the document they are writing, the Constitution, will not itself govern the country. It only sets down the fundamental rules for government. The governing will be done by human beings. In other words, either these delegates figure out how to lure the best and the brightest into office, or the country will be in trouble before the ink dries on the Constitution. You could almost hear these men collectively sigh and ask, "Yes, but tell us how to do it."

Wednesday
August 15, 1787

A KING FOR America? Before you laugh at the thought, read today's *Pennsylvania Gazette*. It says some people in this country are clamoring for a king. On the face of it, that's absurd. Americans fought a long war to be free of the British king. And these delegates are meeting right now to create a *republican* form of government, chosen by the people and accountable to the people. But the rumors can't be dismissed. There *are* those who want a royal government, not a republican one. And right now an anonymous letter is circulating in the country:

> *We have found by experience that we have not wit enough to govern ourselves—that all our declamation about Liberty and the Rights of Man are mere stuff and nonsense. It is high time for us to tread back the wayward path we have walked.*

The writer of that letter wants to send to England for the second son of King George III, who is known as the Bishop of Osnaburg, and have *him* crowned King of America. And the plot is nothing to scoff at. After all, as many as a third of all Americans did not support the Revolution. They remained loyal to the British monarch and cheered for the redcoats. To this day some may still be Tories at heart. So the editor of the *Gazette* had this to say of the rumors:

This plan, we are told, gains friends and partisans rapidly, and it surely is necessary for the great body of the people to be on guard. The Federal Convention may save us from this worst of curses (a Royal Government), if we are wise enough to adopt their recommendations when they shall be communicated to us.

At this point the public has no idea what the convention will recommend. The delegates have stuck to the vow they made back in May not to release any details of their deliberations until they have a final document. But don't forget, they *are* politicians. They listen to public opinion. They care about the public mind. And they've been getting letters asking, "Is it true? Are you really considering a king?"

So the rumors of monarchy must be dealt with. The result is an item in today's *Gazette*, the first and only officially sanctioned leak from the convention. "Though we cannot affirmatively tell you what we are doing," it says, "we can negatively tell you what we are not doing. We never once thought of a King." The Bishop of Osnaburg can unpack.

Thursday
August 16, 1787

THEIR FACES SHOW it. These men are tired. They've been here in Philadelphia for three months now. They're impatient to finish and go home. Such sentiments fill the letters they are writing to family and friends. Here's a letter from James McHenry of Maryland to his wife Peggy:

> *It is extremely distressing to me to remain a day longer in this place, where I find no enjoyments whatever. The only consolation is a hope that my stay will be of shorter duration than I have suggested, when I look to home to repay me for the sacrifice I am making of my happiness.*

And John Dickinson of Delaware to *his* wife, Polly:

> *It is expected, we shall finish about the middle of September, when I hope the sight of you and our dear, dear Children in Health will give me inexpressible Delight.*

Not only are they homesick, they also have businesses to look after and financial affairs to tend. They serve here without salary. The individual states pay their expenses only. And some don't have the wealth to manage indefinitely. Richard Dobbs Spaight will write to a friend in North Carolina that he doesn't even have the money to get home.

My situation here is extremely distressing as I expected when I came away only to stay six weeks or two months. I made a money provision merely for that term. I hope to get away provided I can get money to pay off my accounts here and bear my expenses home.

Some have left already, returning to practice law or manage their farms or businesses. Only the most faithful hang on, three dozen or so who will see this task to its end. They meet six hours a day, six days a week, hammering away at a plan of government, arguing, trading, compromising. It takes great fortitude to keep going. Fortitude and something else. Here's Hugh Williamson of North Carolina writing to the governor of his state:

Colonel Blount and myself are determined to persevere until the business is finished. We owe this duty to the State, and we owe it to the feelings of your Excellency. It will be sufficient for us if we have the satisfaction of believing that we have contributed to the happiness of Millions.

The happiness of millions. It's not just fortitude that keeps them here. It's also faith.

Friday
August 17, 1787

THE CONVENTION TOOK very little time today to dispose of a very large topic: war. Who should be able to declare war? Who should be able to end it? The first draft of the Constitution grants the "power to make war" to both houses of Congress. But Charles Pinckney of South Carolina thinks that's a bad idea. He wants to give the power of war to the Senate alone:

> *The House of Representatives will be too numerous for such deliberations. Its proceedings are too slow. The Senate will be the best depository, being more acquainted with foreign affairs, and most capable of proper resolutions.*

Pinckney's South Carolina colleague Pierce Butler had another idea. He moved to take the power to make war out of the legislative branch altogether:

> *I am for vesting the power in the President, who will have all the requisite qualities and will not make war but when the Nation will support it.*

But that idea brought Elbridge Gerry of Massachusetts to his feet, shocked:

I never expected to hear in a republic a motion to empower the Executive alone to declare war.

And George Mason of Virginia agreed:

I am against giving the power of war to the Executive, because he is not safely to be trusted with it—or to the Senate because it is not so constructed to be entitled to it. I am for clogging rather than facilitating war. I am for facilitating peace.

Keep in mind that these delegates are trying to create a government that answers to the people. Too well they know the example of kings of Europe who go to war at the drop of a royal hat or for the lust of a royal heart. George Mason struck the right note with them when he said they should "clog" the avenue to war and make the government think twice before taking that ultimate step. And yet they know the question of war is not just a theoretical one. Right now there are threats to the United States on all sides. The new government has to be able to defend itself, and the President alone can act quickly and decisively. So the delegates compromised, as usual, with an eye to checks-and-balances. As matters stand now only the Senate has the power to make treaties of peace. Today they gave Congress the power to declare war legally, but they left the President free to repel sudden attacks. Oliver Ellsworth of Connecticut neatly summed up the judgment of the delegates: "It should be more easy to get out of war then into it."

Monday
August 20, 1787

Aʟʟ ʙᴜᴛ ᴛᴡᴏ of the thirteen states have religious qualifications for public office. In Massachusetts and Maryland
you must be a Christian to hold office. New Hampshire, New
Jersey, the Carolinas and Georgia require you to be a Protestant Christian. Even in free-thinking Pennsylvania, you
must believe in God and the divine inspiration of the Scriptures. In Delaware you must also believe in the Trinity. So
these delegates might be expected to write into the new Constitution requirements like those of the states. Jonas Phillips,
for one, certainly thinks they will. And the idea disturbs him.
The delegates will receive an urgent letter from Phillips:

> *I am one of the people called Jews of the City of Philadel-*
> *phia. To swear and believe that the New Testament was*
> *given by divine inspiration is absolutely against the Reli-*
> *gious principle of a Jew and is against his Conscience to*
> *take any such oath.*

He thinks it would be unfair to require religious oaths,

especially considering how Jews were "true and faithful" patriots:

> *During the late Contest with England, they have been foremost in assisting the States with their lives and fortunes. They have supported the Cause, have bravely fought and bled for liberty—which they cannot enjoy.*

Jonas Phillips goes on to say he hopes to live under a government where all religions are on an equal footing, and he ends his letter with a prayer:

> *May the people of these States rise up as a great and young lion. May God extend peace to them and their seed after them so long as the sun and moon endureth.*

Jonas Phillips has no way of knowing that even as he writes, the delegates are taking a revolutionary step. The convention includes some notable champions of religious liberty. They believe the choice of faith is a private matter, even for a public man. So there was hardly an eyebrow raised today when Charles Pinckney of South Carolina offered this proposal to the convention:

> *No religious test or qualification shall ever be annexed to any oath of office under the authority of the United States.*

If these men eventually vote this into the proposed Constitution, they will have set the new American government on a course radically different from the past. And they will have made it possible for Jonas Phillips to serve his country as well as his God.

Tuesday
August 21, 1787

WHAT ABOUT THE defense of the United States? How
will the new national government provide for it? The answer
seems simple. Create an army, a full-time force of soldiers.
But that simple idea sends chills down the spines of many
Americans, including some of these delegates. Listen to Elbridge Gerry of Massachusetts:

> *An army is dangerous in time of peace. I propose that there
> shall not be kept up in time of peace more than three thou-
> sand troops.*

Say the word "army" and most Americans don't think of
security. They think of tyranny and oppression. Throughout
history, monarchs have used armies against the people, to
crush opposition and enforce obedience. King George III
had an army right here not too long ago, in peacetime. Troops
were quartered in American homes and opened fire on
American civilians. That was one of the chief grievances in
the Declaration of Independence:

He has kept among us, in times of peace, Standing Armies without the Consent of our legislatures. He has affected to render the Military independent of and superior to the Civil power.

After America's own Continental Army sent the redcoats packing, Congress disbanded it. Americans feel safest relying on their own neighbors for defense, on the local militia companies, civilians all, who practice with the rifle only when they've finished with the plow.

Yet the delegates know they inhabit a dangerous continent. The United States is young, and predators stalk it. Could a few half-baked companies of half-trained farmers really defend the country against a surprise attack by Spain or Great Britain? General Washington doesn't say much at this convention, but the old Commander in Chief knows a little something about fighting. So when Elbridge Gerry moved to limit the army to three thousand troops, the General reportedly nudged a colleague and whispered a motion of his own. He suggested that no foreign enemy should invade the United States with more than three thousand troops.

The General's joke was off the record, but it wasn't off the mark. The delegates put aside their doubts and decided the government *should* maintain a standing army. But they will give supreme command of that army to the President, who will be a civilian. And they'll give power over its purse to the Congress, accountable to the people. That should keep the army from one day standing *against* the country instead of *for* it.

Wednesday
August 22, 1787

FOR A MOMENT today you might have thought an Old Testament prophet had seized the floor of this convention. The language was biblical, the wrath and sorrow from Amos and Isaiah. But the voice belonged to George Mason and the accent was unmistakably Virginian. Though Mason himself is a slaveowner, he spoke on the evil of slavery. And like those prophets of old, he warned that evil has its consequences:

> *Slaves bring the judgment of heaven on a Country. As nations cannot be rewarded or punished in the next world, they must be in this. By an inevitable chain of causes and effects, Providence punishes national sins, by national calamities.*

Mason would like to see slavery eliminated altogether—but that wasn't the topic before the convention today. The subject was the slave trade. Should the new Constitution put limits on bringing more slaves into this country? No, said John Rutledge of South Carolina. Emphatically no!

> *If the Convention thinks that North Carolina, South Carolina, and Georgia will ever agree to the plan, unless their right to import slaves is untouched, the expectation is vain. The people of those States will never be such fools as to give up so important an interest.*

That's reality, said Charles Cotesworth Pinckney. Even if *he* were convinced that slavery is evil, it would make no difference in South Carolina:

> *If I and all my colleagues were to sign the Constitution, and use our personal influence, it would be of no avail towards obtaining the assent of our Constituents. South Carolina and Georgia cannot do without slaves.*

Those states are demanding a guarantee in the Constitution that Congress will never outlaw or even tax the slave trade. If they don't get this guarantee, they say, they'll walk out of the convention. This leads the practical men of New England, men such as Connecticut's Roger Sherman, to consider politics before principle:

> *I disapprove of the slave trade. Yet, as it is expedient to have as few objections as possible to the proposed scheme of Government, I think it best to leave the matter as we find it.*

A committee has been appointed to search for a compromise. But here in this hall, after all the delegates have gone, you can hear echoes of the angry debate. The defiance of the deep South—never, never, never! And the melancholy prophecy of Mason—that national sins will be punished by national calamities.

Thursday
August 23, 1787

IF GEORGE MASON had his way, it would be unconstitutional to overeat, overspend, or overdress. The Virginian proposed giving Congress the power to make "sumptuary laws" that prohibit extravagant spending on luxuries. In Mason's opinion, what's at stake is the very survival of the republic:

> *No free Government, or the blessing of liberty, can be preserved to any people but by a firm adherence to justice, moderation, temperance, frugality, and virtue, and by frequent recurrence to fundamental principles.*

Mason is no eccentric. He may wash his head in cold water every morning. He writes testy letters home complaining about the silly social whirl here in Philadelphia. But he's not alone in believing that a popular taste for extravagance could eventually destroy this country. That passage about frugality and virtue comes from one of the most honored documents in America, the Declaration of Rights of Virginia, which Mason wrote in 1776. And it reflects one of the most enduring of American political traditions: that the nation will be strong and blessed only as long as its people are virtuous. It's a simple equation. America is a republic. A republic is based on the people and dedicated to the common good. If the people put the common good before their own selfish interest, the republic flourishes. If they pursue only private gain, the republic dies. So nothing could be more selfish, more un-American, than for citizens to amass great wealth and spend it on themselves. Another delegate, John Dickinson of Delaware, said as much one day at the convention. He was arguing against the proposal to require that holders of public office own a minimum amount of property:

> *I doubt the policy of interweaving into a Republican constitution a veneration for wealth. I have always understood that a veneration for poverty and virtue were the objects of Republican encouragement.*

So the idea that prudence and sacrifice are essential to the country is rooted in a philosophy of politics that goes back to ancient days. But America keeps growing and changing. People who came here to be free increasingly want to live their lives as they please. George Mason's proposal for sumptuary laws to regulate private behavior found no favor and was voted down. The new Constitution will make America safe for extravagance.

Friday
August 24, 1787

IMAGINE *YOU* ARE a member of this convention. Not an observer, reporter, or outsider, but a *delegate*, sent here by your state to help write a new constitution for America. Remember—the present government isn't working. It can't pay it's debts. Congress can't keep peace among the states. The nation is virtually helpless against foreign enemies. The country's greatest hero, George Washington, has said the Union is falling apart, and many leading citizens agree. That's why you're here: to write a constitution that will create a new national government strong enough to save the country.

You and the other delegates have worked all summer. You have the rough draft of a new constitution. You're down to the finishing touches. One of the most difficult issues, how the states will be represented in Congress, has been settled by compromise. You have also compromised on counting slaves for the purpose of representation. But the slavery issue won't go away. South Carolina and Georgia are threatening to walk out unless the convention guarantees that the new Constitution will allow them to keep importing slaves. Their economies depend on huge numbers of slaves to grow rice, tobacco, and indigo. The work is backbreaking. Slaves die young, and plantation owners want to keep the supply coming. That's why South Carolina and Georgia are demanding that the Constitution include an explicit clause forbidding the new government from interfering with the slave trade. Their demand has the convention in knots. Edmund Randolph of Virginia put it this way:

> The Convention is in a dilemma. By agreeing to the clause, it will revolt the Quakers, the Methodists and many others in the States having no slaves. On the other hand, two States might be lost to the Union.

No one here hates the slave trade more than Gouverneur Morris of Pennsylvania. To him it's an odious institution, "the curse of heaven." But Morris is a practical man too. He wants the northern and southern states to strike a bargain. And that's what was proposed today. Let the slave trade continue for now, but after 1800, let Congress put a stop to it if it will. There's your choice: union with slavery, or slavery without union. You're a delegate. How will you choose?

Monday
August 27, 1787

THEY ARGUED FOR days about the powers of the presidency. They fought for weeks over representation in Congress. But when they finally got around to the judiciary, the delegates disposed of it in a very little time and almost without debate.

It's not that they think the courts unimportant. When Thomas Jefferson drafted the Declaration of Independence eleven years ago, he included the weakness of the colonial judicial system in the long list of complaints about King George:

He has made Judges dependent on his Will alone, for the tenure of their offices, and the amount and payment of their salaries.

So it didn't take the delegates any time today to agree on the most fundamental point. The courts must be independent, truly a third branch of government separate and distinct from the other two. But how can they ensure that independence? One way is for judges to serve "during good behavior.'' That will usually mean ''for life''—no one will be able to fire them arbitrarily. That's agreed to today. Another is to guarantee that judges' salaries can't be cut while they're in office, which means they won't be punished in the pocketbook for unpopular decisions. Agreed. But they still have to resolve the harder question: Who should choose the judges? The proposal on the table now leaves it up to the Senate. But Nathaniel Gorham of Massachusetts thinks the President would be more responsible than senators:

The executive would certainly be more answerable for a good appointment, as the whole blame of a bad one would fall on him alone. I do not mean that he would be answerable under any other penalty than that of public censure, which with honorable minds is a sufficient one.

Yes, said James Madison of Virginia, let the President name the judges. But make sure the Senate agrees:

This would unite the advantage of responsibility in the Executive with the security afforded in the second branch against any incautious or corrupt nomination by the Executive.

Madison's idea will prevail. The delegates decide they can best guarantee the independence of the judicial branch by making both of the other branches responsible for choosing it.

It's a simple outline they agree on for the judiciary. There will be one Supreme Court of the United States and lesser courts that Congress can create as needed. Beyond that, the judicial branch will have to be defined over time. But this much is clear. It will be separate from the other two branches. Separate, but equal.

Tuesday
August 28, 1787

W<small>HEN AN</small> A<small>MERICAN</small> gets paid for something in 1787, he wants to be paid in good hard coins of gold or silver. He's skeptical about taking the paper money printed by the states. He just doesn't trust it. Neither do most of the delegates at this federal convention, and they aren't afraid to say so. The recent proposal to let the national government print its own paper money absolutely scandalized Oliver Ellsworth of Connecticut:

> *This is a favorable moment to shut and bar the door against paper money. The mischiefs of the various experiments which have been made are now fresh in the public mind and have excited the disgust of all the respectable part of America.*

George Read of Delaware said the proposal for paper money is "as alarming as the mark of the Beast in Revelation." So it was struck out.

Why such passion? After all, there is a real shortage of gold and silver money. The states and Confederation government are too broke to mint any. There's not enough cash to keep the economy healthy, and merchants have to make do with a scarce supply of foreign coins. So it doesn't seem to make much sense to outlaw paper money.

But these delegates all lived through the frenzied finance of the Revolution. Forty-two times the Continental Congress went to the printers and poured out millions in paper currency. Its value fell and fell until the harshest thing to say about a product was that it "wasn't worth a continental." The states also printed millions, so that in Virginia alone it took five thousand dollars in local money to buy a pair of shoes. The soldiers and farmers and merchants who got paid with this paper were, in effect, robbed by their governments. No wonder raw nerves are touched.

Yet there's another side to the story. Although that worthless wallpaper of revolutionary days ruined individuals, it saved the Republic. It bought supplies and muskets and beef for the army. That's why George Mason of Virginia isn't quite sure he wants a permanent prohibition:

I have a mortal hatred of paper money. Yet as I cannot foresee all emergencies, I am unwilling to tie the hands of the Legislature. The late war could not have been carried on had such a prohibition existed.

He loses. The majority of delegates, for the moment, thinks that giving any legislature the right to print even a little paper money is like giving a drunkard just a little sip. For now, they will try to keep Congress sober.

Wednesday
August 29, 1787

T HEY'RE TRYING TO write a constitution for the United States of America, but today the delegates were thinking about the free state of Franklin. That's right—the free state of Franklin. It wasn't one of the thirteen colonies and it isn't one of the thirteen states of the Union. But might it become the fourteenth?

North Carolina has long claimed control over the Tennessee Territory. But three years ago some pioneers out in the remote Tennessee River Valley decided the state government wasn't looking out for their interests. So they seceded. Asking nobody's consent they carved out a prime chunk of wilderness and declared it the free and independent state of Franklin. They elected a governor, set up a militia, and provided for the collection of taxes. Those taxes are payable in tobacco, fruit and brandy, or beeswax since nobody has much hard currency on the frontier. Now Franklin is eager to join the Union as a state in its own right.

So what's the problem? Well, there's all that tax revenue North Carolina would lose, all that brandy and beeswax. There's national security. Some Franklinites are muttering:

If the Union doesn't want us, maybe the Spanish across the Mississippi will. And there's the principle of the thing. What if other counties also decided they didn't like North Carolina's ways, and went the same way as the state of Franklin? What state wants to see itself slowly dismembered by its own citizens? It's enough to drive a proud state to civil war. There was a not-so-veiled threat to that effect by the governor of North Carolina a while back:

If no other ways are found to save the state's honor but this last sad expedient, she may regain her Government over the revolted territory or render it not worth possessing.

Now you see why the delegates have been preoccupied with the free state of Franklin, and other territories such as Vermont and Kentucky that also want to join the Union. Do they write a constitution that admits new states on the same terms with the first thirteen? In principle, yes. James Madison reasoned this way:

The Western States neither would nor ought to submit to a Union which degrades them from equal rank with the other States.

But what's to prevent every band of disgruntled citizens from bolting their state, proclaiming independence, and asking for admission to the Union? The delegates came up with a solution. New states *will* have the same rights and privileges as old ones. But no new state can be created inside another without the consent of Congress and the state legislatures concerned. In other words, all states are created equal. Provided they first get permission.

Thursday
August 30, 1787

UNTIL TODAY THERE was absolutely no mention of religion in the proposed Constitution of the United States. It isn't that the men writing the Constitution aren't religious. Some are and some aren't. But they all seem to agree on one thing. A person's religious beliefs are not the business of the national government and certainly shouldn't be a prerequisite for holding national office. Charles Pinckney of South Carolina has already moved to make that clear in the Constitution:

> *No religious test shall ever be required as a qualification to any office or public trust under the authority of the United States.*

The delegates returned to the proposal today and it passed unanimously. The only word of protest came from Roger Sherman of Connecticut. He said he wasn't sure they needed even *that* guarantee:

I think it is unnecessary. The prevailing liberality is a sufficient security against such tests.

This is quite a switch from colonial days. The Puritans came here to worship the way they wanted to. But they didn't have much tolerance for anyone who worshipped differently. Dissenters could be thrown in jail. Or chased out of town. Or worse. Most of the colonies had "established churches," and some of the states still do. That means a specific church is sanctioned by the government, and people have to pay taxes to support it whether they belong to that church or not. This infuriates Thomas Jefferson, and he wrote his fury into Virginia's Statute of Religious Freedom:

Almighty God hath created the mind free. To compel a man to furnish contributions of money for the propagation of opinions which he disbelieves and abhors is sinful and tyrannical. No man shall be compelled to frequent or support any religious Worship whatsoever.

Over the years religious tolerance has grown in America. Still, the country is overwhelmingly Protestant. There are fewer than 2,000 Jews in the country and about 25,000 Catholics. That's why George Washington's action on the first Sunday of the convention was so significant. He went to a Roman Catholic Mass. Washington is an Episcopalian. He is also a politician, and he knows the value of a symbol. This was his way of signaling an open-mindedness about religion. In this new country, religious tolerance—in fact, religious freedom—will be the only official creed.

Friday
August 31, 1787

THE CONSTITUTION MUST be almost finished, because the delegates have stopped debating what's *in* it long enough to debate what happens *to* it when they're done. It's one of the most critical decisions they'll make all summer. How many of the thirteen states will have to ratify the Constitution before it takes effect?

JAMES WILSON: *Seven. That is a majority.*
ROGER SHERMAN: *Ten states, at least.*
EDMUND RANDOLPH: *Nine. That is a respectable majority.*

Daniel Carroll of Maryland would not have that. He said only one number is possible. It's all or nothing.

Fill in the blank with "the thirteen." Unanimity is necessary to dissolve the existing confederacy.

Carroll argued that all thirteen states agreed to the Articles of Confederation, the charter of the present government, and all thirteen would have to approve any changes. Anything less would be mutiny. But Carroll's proposal would kill the new Constitution in its cradle. Rhode Island didn't even bother to come to this convention. That's one negative vote for certain. There's also strong opposition in New York and Maryland. So the delegates agreed on the number nine, "a respectable majority."

But there's another question: Should the Constitution be ratified by the state legislatures or by special conventions of the people? Elbridge Gerry is already on record: Not the people; "they have the wildest ideas of government in the world." But Nathaniel Gorham, Gerry's colleague from Massachusetts, disagreed. Leave it to the legislatures, he said, and local politicians, who benefit from the system as it is, will surely find some way to block ratification. Two Virginians, George Mason and James Madison, have already argued that the choice *must* be made by the people:

Referring the plan to the authority of the people is essential. The Legislatures have no power to ratify it. They are the mere creatures of the State Constitutions, and cannot be greater than their creators.

I consider the difference between a system founded on the Legislatures only, and one founded on the people, to be the true difference between a league or treaty and a Constitution.

The issue is settled. The people in special conventions, not the legislatures, will decide if the Constitution shall live or die. Madison said that by resorting to the people, all difficulties are overcome. It's an article of faith to him, one he has expressed over and over at this convention. It will soon be tested.

Saturday
September 1, 1787

*P*HILADELPHIA, SEPTEMBER 1, 1787. *I am distressed,*
my dearest Girl, at the notice of your indisposition. I would
not remain here two hours was I not under a necessity of
staying to prevent my colleagues from saying that I broke
up the representation.

That's Elbridge Gerry, delegate from Massachusetts, writing home to his wife, Ann. The other delegates know him as stubborn and contrary, with a nervous twitch to his eye. They dislike his constant grumbling and say he opposes everything he hasn't proposed himself. But grumbling Gerry has a surprising private side. He is a doting newlywed. Last year, just shy of forty-two, he was married. His bride is twenty years old, rich, educated, and rumored to be the most beautiful woman in the United States. Gerry misses her passionately.

If anything makes life in the least desirable it is you, my
dearest girl. Detached from your comforts, life to me would
be a source of evils. I am as sick of being here as you can
conceive.

160

By now everybody is sick of being here, but Gerry may be the most desperate. He's confided to his wife that he will not sign the Constitution, and he foresees nothing but dissension throughout the country when the plan is released.

I am exceedingly distressed at the proceedings of the convention, and almost sure they will lay the foundation of a civil War. Had I known what would have happened, nothing would have induced me to come here.

Gerry would like to leave. He's worried about the health of his wife and their baby daughter in New York. The climate there is a little healthier than Philadelphia's. Every day here you can see the bodies of small children carried through these streets. But summer can be deadly in any city where disease festers. Gerry fills his letters to Ann with advice about proper care for herself and the baby.

Take Rhubarb two or three evenings successively, and drink gruel morning and evening with cold camomile tea. . . . Guard against the Coolness and dampness of Mornings and Evenings, and also the house when washed. The baby should not be carried in a Room the day it is washed.

Elbridge Gerry takes his seat in the State House every day. He thinks of civil war and damp rooms; of his public duty and his young wife; of this republic, its fate . . . and camomile tea. He's very much a character, Gerry: signer of the Declaration of Independence and a worry-wart. It's typical of these men who are creating a nation and thinking of home.

Monday
September 3, 1787

GENERAL CHARLES COTESWORTH Pinckney had a confession to make. The soldier from South Carolina recently told his fellow delegates here that he used to have "prejudices" against New Englanders. Now he's willing to admit they can be as liberal and candid as anyone.

It's telling testimony for what it reveals of the obstacles that lie beyond this convention. If these delegates can create a constitution, can the constitution create a nation? America in 1787 isn't one nation, indivisible. It's more like thirteen little realms, each with its own native pride and prejudice. They don't trust each other, in part because they are so outrageously opinionated about each other. The Yankees from New England are looked upon by the rest of the country as intolerant, self-righteous, and as cunning as the very devil. When Gouverneur Morris was growing up in New York, his father wrote in his will that the boy should receive the best education possible—with one restriction:

> *My Express Directions are that he be never sent for that purpose to Connecticut, lest he should imbibe in his youth*

that low Craft and cunning so Incident to the People of that Country.

And how do Pennsylvania mothers scare their children into obedience? Better be good, they say, or we'll give you away to the Yankees. Of course these prejudices between states and regions come on top of divisive economic issues. The differences are so deep that an English clergyman named Josiah Tucker, who considers himself a friend of America, had this to say about the new country:

The mutual antipathies and clashing interests of the Americans . . . indicate they will have no centre of union and no common interest. They never can be united into one compact empire under any species of government whatever; a disunited people till the end of time, suspicious and distrustful of each other, they will be divided and subdivided into little commonwealths.

And listen to the American patriot John Adams. All people love their country, he once said. But the affection grows as they get closer to home:

It is stronger and stronger, as we descend to the County, Town, Parish, Neighborhood, and Family, which we call our own. And here we find it often so powerful as to become partial, to blind our eyes, to darken our understandings and pervert our wills.

How then are these thirteen little realms to avoid the endless squabbling that brought ruin to the republics of ancient Greece and the city-states of medieval Italy? More than a change of government is required. The Constitution will also have to create in people a change of heart.

Tuesday
September 4, 1787

INDIANS, THE PEOPLE who were in America first, have barely been mentioned at this federal convention. That's not to say the Indians are far from the delegates' minds. In fact how to deal with the Indians is one of the gravest issues facing this nation—and one of the prime reasons the convention was called. Ever since the European settlers arrived on these shores, the encounters with the Indians have become more and more heartbreaking. Just look at what's happening right now down in Georgia. Only the easternmost edge of the state is settled; the rest belongs to the Creek tribes. But settlers covet the rich Indian territory. So they've been making treaties to get it, without authorization from the current Congress. Congress protests. Congress issues statements. Congress studies the matter. Just last month a committee reported that pure greed on the part of the white settlers is to blame for the whole situation:

An avaricious disposition to acquire large tracts of land and often by unfair means appears to be the principal source of difficulties with the Indians.

But Congress also declares its good intentions:

The utmost good faith shall always be observed towards the Indians; their lands and property shall never be taken from them without their consent . . . Laws founded in justice and humanity shall from time to time, be made, for preventing the wrongs being done to them, and for preserving peace and friendship with them.

For all its fine words about good faith and justice, Congress hasn't been able to guarantee either. It doesn't have the power to stop the Georgians from doing as they please within their own state. Meanwhile, the Indians are fighting back, with attacks and raids, and they're making treaties with the Spanish. Rumor has it one hundred horseloads of arms and supplies were recently sent from Spanish Florida. That situation could lead to war with Spain, and now Georgia is calling for help.

The situation is chaotic, and Congress can't do anything without authority and power to back it up. That's why the new Constitution specifies that only the national government can make treaties with other nations. That's why the delegates voted today to give the new Congress, not the states, the power to regulate commerce with ''foreign Nations and Indian Tribes.'' Foreign nations and Indian tribes. There's something inevitable and sad about the phrase. The people who were here first are now officially and finally recognized as a foreign nation.

Wednesday
September 5, 1787

DESPERATE TIMES BREED desperate measures. The delegates have so despaired over the method of electing the President that this week they settled on something called the "electoral college." It's an ungainly creature, and has about it the look and smell of compromise. But you can't blame them for throwing their hands up. They've argued through at least seven different schemes for electing the executive, taken dozens of votes, and found fatal flaws in each suggestion. Each time they arrive at an impasse they feel the frustration expressed by James Wilson of Pennsylvania:

> *This subject has greatly divided the House. It is in truth the most difficult of all on which we have had to decide. I have never made up an opinion on it entirely to my own satisfaction.*

So—compromise. An electoral college. Here's how it works: Each state will appoint as many electors as it has members of the House and Senate. Each elector will vote for two candidates. The candidate with the most votes will be

President. The one who comes in second will be Vice President. And if no one gets a clear majority, the House of Representatives will pick the President.

It sounds complicated, and awkward. But the delegates think it's better than the alternatives already considered. Election by Congress would violate the whole idea of separation of powers; the President would be too much at the mercy of the men who put him in office. But letting the people elect the President directly is hardly realistic. How could the voters in a country this big ever know enough about candidates from faraway states? Electors, on the other hand, will have time to weigh the merits of candidates, to remain a step removed from popular passions. It sounds rational. Yet the delegates are far from enthusiastic about it:

> ABRAHAM BALDWIN: *The plan is not so objectionable when well considered, as at first view.*

> PIERCE BUTLER: *The mode is not free from objections, but much more so than an election by the Legislature.*

> ALEXANDER HAMILTON: *I mean to support the plan to be recommended, as better than nothing.*

The plan for an electoral college does have one obvious advantage over the others. It's on the table right now. They can take it and move on. If they reject it they have to start over. They take it. Sometimes at this convention, compromise means being too tired to argue any more.

Thursday
September 6, 1787

Now you see it, now you don't. That's been the case at this convention all summer. The delegates approve a proposal and then take it back. This week they agreed on a plan for the presidency contrary to almost everything they had already decided. Creating the presidency has been one of their biggest headaches. They fear that if the Constitution gives the President too much power, he could end up a monarch or a tyrant. But if his powers are limited, he might not be able to govern effectively.

Until this week, most of the delegates feared tyranny more than inefficiency. That's understandable. These men have lived under kings and governors, but never a president. No one has ever seen a president, so no one knows what one might do once in office. He could turn into a king as naturally as a tadpole becomes a frog. Benjamin Franklin said as much back in June:

> *It will be said that we don't propose to establish Kings. I know it. But there is a natural inclination in mankind to Kingly Government. I am apprehensive, therefore, that the*

Government of these States, may in future times, end in a Monarchy.

Given such fears, it's not surprising most delegates kept right on voting to weaken the president. He was to have an imperial title, "Your Excellency," but so little real power one had to wonder what he would do all day. And Congress would have just the opposite problem: too much to do. Congress would conduct foreign policy, declare war, appoint ambassadors, pick the Supreme Court. Congress would even choose His Excellency, the President.

But suddenly this week all that changed. A special committee that had been instructed to study the matter returned with a report that completely reinvented the President. He is a weakling no longer. Now *he* will be empowered to make treaties, appoint justices, and name ambassadors, all with the approval of the Senate. He is to be elected not by Congress but by an electoral college, and he can stand for reelection as many times as he wishes. It appears that his powers have been left so open he'll be able to make the office what he wants it to be.

It's difficult to say why this turnabout occurred. The delegates fear monarchy as much as ever. But they've been saying all summer they want to create a government based on the popular will and carried out by three branches which can prevent one another from going too far. If they've done their work well, Congress, the courts, the people, and the Constitution will prevent "Your Excellency" from becoming "Your Majesty."

Friday
September 7, 1787

They're acting swiftly now. This convention has one eye on its unfinished business and the other on adjournment. The delegates have just about settled the matter of the presidency, so now they are turning to the Vice President. According to the proposal now on the table, his main duty will be to serve as president of the Senate, voting only when he's needed to break a tie. But some of the delegates think that's totally improper. It confuses two distinct branches of government, the legislative and the executive. How can they check one another if they blend into a single office whose occupant is neither fish nor fowl? Here's George Mason of Virginia:

> *The office of Vice President is an encroachment on the rights of the Senate. It mixes the Legislative and Executive, which ought to be kept as separate as possible.*

Elbridge Gerry of Massachusetts was even more emphatic. The Vice President should *not* serve as President of the Senate:

We might as well put the President himself at the head of the Legislature. It is absolutely improper. I am against having any Vice President.

But Roger Sherman of Connecticut disagreed. He said they have to give the poor man something to do other than inquire into the President's health:

If the Vice president were not to be President of the Senate, he would be without employment.

And no one wants an unemployed Vice President. So the delegates agreed: The Vice President *will* be president of the Senate.

As these men begin to conclude their work, they wonder more and more often how the public will react to this new Constitution when it's finally published. Just this week, James Madison revealed some of his own apprehensions in a letter to his friend Thomas Jefferson, the American Minister to France:

Reports and conjectures abound concerning the nature of the plan which is to be proposed. The public however is certainly in the dark with regard to it. The Convention is equally in the dark as to the reception which may be given to it on its publication. It may well be expected that certain characters will wage war against any reform whatever. If the present moment be lost, it is hard to say what may be our fate.

The reckoning approaches. There are last-minute votes to take, details to nail down. But their work is almost done. They look up from it now to consider the judgment of the people—the judgment that could decide if they labored this summer in vain.

Monday
September 10, 1787

W HAT IF THIS Constitution turns out to be less than perfect? It's a reasonable possibility, and these men have thought about it. They also know times change, and future generations will face needs that cannot be foreseen now. So they agree. The Constitution should contain some mechanism by which it can be amended. George Mason of Virginia stated the principle back in June:

> *The plan now to be formed will certainly be defective, as the Confederation has been found on trial to be. Amendments, therefore, will be necessary, and it will be better to provide for them in an easy, regular, and constitutional way, than to trust to chance and violence.*

So the Constitution will be amendable—but how? If they make the amendment process too easy, the Constitution might be changed by every gust of popular passion. If they make it too difficult, the Constitution might be so inflexible the people will be afraid to ratify it. The most recent proposal gives state legislatures the power to suggest amendments. But today Alexander Hamilton, who has returned to the convention, objected to that idea and offered one of his own:

The State Legislatures will not apply for alterations, but with a view to increase their own powers. The National Legislature will be the first to perceive and will be most sensible to the necessity of amendments.

As usual, the delegates compromised. Congress will be able to propose amendments, and so will the state legislatures. Either way, no amendment will go into effect until it's been approved by three-quarters of the states. It won't be easy to change the Constitution, but it will be possible.

Except in one respect. You'll recall that some weeks ago the small states, on threat of walking out, forced the large states to give them equality in the Senate. The hard-fought compromise says that each state, regardless of size, will have two senators. Now the small states demand an insurance policy in the Constitution. They want a provision that the arrangement can't be changed without their consent. The large states capitulate. Here at the end they don't want a fight that could tear the convention apart. It means there's one provision of the Constitution that's almost certain never to be amended.

Tuesday
September 11, 1787

Day in and day out the delegates keep working. They're inventing a new government that will affect every citizen of the country. But the proceedings have been kept entirely secret. And the public doesn't know what kind of government these men will recommend. All the people can do is wait—and speculate. The stakes are high. One newspaper says the anticipation has brought the country to a virtual standstill:

> *Every enterprise, public as well as private, seems suspended till it is known what kind of Government we are to receive from our National Convention. The States neglect their roads and canals, till they see whether those necessary improvements will not become the objects of a National Government. Trading companies suspend their voyages, till they see how far their commerce will be protected and promoted by a National system of commercial regulations.*

With so much at stake there's been surprisingly little effort by outsiders to lobby the delegates, little pressure to influence the outcome. It's the reputation of the delegates that has assured their freedom of action this summer. The country might not have been so patient with an assembly of lesser men, or so willing to let them work in secrecy. But the men here are considered by most of the public to be beyond suspicion. A local newspaper recently put it this way:

> *The members of the Convention are entitled to the universal confidence of the people of America. Such a body of enlightened and honest men perhaps never before met for political purposes in any country upon the face of the earth.*

Not only Americans care what's happening here, or have a stake in it. Here's another article that's been showing up in newspapers:

> *The oppressed and persecuted in every country look with great eagerness to the United States. Should the new Federal Government be adopted, thousands would embark immediately for America. Germany and Ireland would send colonies of cultivators of the earth; while England and Scotland would fill our towns and cities with industrious mechanics and manufacturers.*

In the Old World, still ruled by kings and priests, the common folk have heard that something radically different struggles to be born in the New World. The men at work here are honest enough to know that the accounts of their virtue are exaggerated. But they're wise enough to know that the hopes of all those millions are not.

Wednesday
September 12, 1787

Here it is—the proposed Constitution of the United States. For the past few days the five members of the Committee of Style have been polishing each clause and comma. They have distilled the work of four months into a document of only four pages. But in those pages is the blueprint of an entirely new government. It's spelled out in seven articles.

Article One. All legislative Powers herein granted shall be vested in a Congress of the United States . . .

All Bills for raising Revenue shall originate in the House of Representatives . . .

Article Two. The executive Power shall be vested in a President . . .

He shall from time to time give to the Congress Information of the State of the Union . . .

Article Three. The judicial Power of the United States, shall be vested in one supreme Court . . .

Article Four. New States may be admitted by the Congress into this Union . . .

Article Five. The Congress . . . shall propose Amendments to this Constitution . . .

Article Six. This Constitution . . . shall be the supreme Law of the Land . . .

Article Seven. The Ratification of the Conventions of nine States shall be sufficient for the Establishment of this Constitution.

It's a model of essential principles stated in spare and simple prose. Most of this final draft apparently came from the pen of Gouverneur Morris, who surprised the others with an eloquent preamble:

We the People of the United States, in Order to form a more perfect Union, establish Justice, insure domestic Tranquility, provide for the common defence, promote the general Welfare, and secure the Blessings of Liberty to ourselves and our Posterity, do ordain and establish this Constitution for the United States of America.

Read the seven articles and you know how the nation is to act as a political body: who is to govern and how, the rights and duties of those in power. Read the preamble, and you are suddenly confronted with a moral compact: ''We the People.'' Here are what these men see as the fundamental laws of the nation, their ideas of the common wealth. No one knows what the disposition of their effort will be, whether the people will accept it. But for the moment at least, this Constitution has taken the collective wisdom of these politicians and patriots and turned it into a single American voice.

Thursday
September 13, 1787

THERE IS THE rumbling of a storm over this convention, a signal of potential trouble—not over what's in the proposed new Constitution, but what isn't. When the delegates gathered yesterday to read over the final draft, George Mason of Virginia said something's missing:

> I wish the plan was prefaced with a Bill of Rights. And I would second a motion if made for the purpose. It would give great quiet to the people.

Freedom of speech, freedom of religion, the right to a fair trial—these and other liberties would be spelled out in a Bill of Rights. Eight of the state constitutions have such guarantees. Mason himself wrote Virginia's. And he said he could draw up a *national* Bill of Rights in just a few hours. Roger Sherman of Connecticut said no, it's just not necessary:

> I am for securing the rights of the people where requisite. But the state Declarations of Rights are not repealed by this Constitution. They are sufficient.

Mason objected. This new Constitution is to be the supreme law of the land. The government could be overzealous, and without a guarantee of their individual liberties people would be at its mercy. He feels this so deeply that he says he will not sign the Constitution unless it does contain a Bill of Rights. But when the question was called, every state present, even Mason's own Virginia, voted against adding a Bill of Rights.

Why? Possibly because the delegates have been here almost four months now and can't bear the thought of prolonging their work. Nor do the southern states want to stir the hound of hypocrisy that slumbers in the corner of this convention. Later, Charles Cotesworth Pinckney of South Carolina will admit quite candidly why he didn't want a Bill of Rights:

> *Such bills generally begin with declaring that all men are by nature born free. Now, we should make that declaration with very bad grace, when a large part of our property consists in men who are actually born slaves.*

But the chief opposition to a Bill of Rights comes from delegates who honestly see no need for it. They point to those progressive state constitutions with their guarantees. The new Constitution limits the power of the national government by spreading it among three branches. The American people just fought a war to secure their rights. Surely they can now— and always—count on Congress or the President or the courts to guard these liberties. Can't they?

Friday
September 14, 1787

In 1776, AT the start of the American Revolution, the patriot John Adams declared this was a great time to be alive. In a pamphlet addressed to his fellow citizens, Adams wrote:

> *You and I, my dear Friend, have been sent into life, at a time when the greatest law-givers of antiquity would have wished to have lived. How few of the human race have ever enjoyed an opportunity of making an election of government for themselves or their children?*

Eleven years later, here in Philadelphia, the delegates to this convention must stop every now and then to remind themselves that is exactly what they're doing. They're choosing a government for themselves and their children and their children's children. It's as if they are putting down the foundation for a great house many generations will live in. As the family grows and changes, new needs will require new rooms. But the foundation is the bedrock, on which the generations build.

Constitution-writing is not a new idea in America. Every

one of the thirteen states began as a colony with a written charter, setting out the basic principles of how government should work and what it could and could not do. The religious protesters who came here early on called this charter a covenant between themselves and God, and a compact among themselves.

With the Revolution of 1776 the colonies declared themselves independent states, and most wrote their own state constitutions. The men at this convention have drawn upon those state constitutions for ideas and language. Look at the one in Massachusetts, which John Adams helped to write:

> All power residing originally in the people, and being derived from them, the several magistrates and officers of government . . . are their substitutes and agents, and are at all times accountable to them.

Few of the men here would disagree with those uncompromising words. One great idea unites them: that government exercises power only in the name of the people and with their consent. Governors are but temporary stewards of the nation's destiny. To put that in writing and make it binding—that's the purpose of a constitution.

Obviously it's not enough just to engross the words on parchment. A philosopher much admired by these men reminds them that any constitution is "a mere dead letter, and the best laws useless if they be not sacredly observed." True enough. But if the foundation is deep and strong, the house may survive its most reckless tenants. Or so these men trust.

Saturday
September 15, 1787

This was the longest session of the entire convention. And one of the most frustrating. The delegates finished writing the Constitution, and this evening approved it as expected. But the hope that every delegate here would support it was shattered by the decision of three men—Randolph, Mason, and Gerry—not to sign the final document.

Edmund Randolph spoke first:

> It pains me to differ from the body of the Convention on the close of the great and awful subject of our labors.

The men listening must have been struck by the irony. Three months ago Randolph had introduced the very proposal, the Virginia Plan, which has become the principal scheme of the proposed Constitution. But as the convention added more and more powers to Congress, Randolph grew alarmed:

> Am I to promote the establishment of a plan which I verily believe will end in tyranny?

Now Governor Randolph says he will sign only if the delegates approve his plan for a *second* convention, giving the people time to study this proposed Constitution and to suggest amendments.

His fellow Virginian George Mason agreed with him.

This Constitution has been formed without the knowledge or idea of the people. It is improper to say to the people, take this or nothing.

It's a radical turnabout for George Mason, too. In July, he declared he would rather ''bury his bones in Philadelphia'' than leave here without a Constitution. But Mason didn't mean just *any* constitution. He is grieved by this one because it does not stop the slave trade, and it does not have a Bill of Rights. Mason now swears he would rather ''cut off his right hand'' than sign a Constitution that could lead to a despotic government.

The third dissenter is Elbridge Gerry of Massachusetts. He gave a long speech saying the new Constitution invests Congress with too many vague and unlimited powers.

But the other delegates were not swayed. They had heard enough debate. Shortly before six o'clock, General Washington called the question. First, on Randolph's proposal that everything be submitted to a second convention: *No.* Then, on whether to agree to the Constitution now before them: *Aye.* It is done. The Constitution will be put to parchment and then be ready for signing.

Monday
September 17, 1787

T HEY ARGUED TO the end. Down to the last minute, the thirty-eight delegates who plan to sign the Constitution were trying to change the minds of the three delegates who say they will not. They want everyone's name on it because the enemies of the Constitution—and there are many—will exploit every division among the men who wrote it. The three dissenters are men of influence: Edmund Randolph and George Mason of Virginia and Elbridge Gerry of Massachusetts. So there were strong and eloquent pleas to make the signing unanimous. Listen to Alexander Hamilton of New York:

> *I am anxious that every member should sign. A few characters of consequence, by opposing or even refusing to sign the Constitution, might do infinite mischief.*

He will sign even though he had argued against many of the convention's proposals. So will Gouverneur Morris of Pennsylvania.

I too have objections. But I will take this Constitution with all its faults. The majority has determined in its favor, and by that determination I shall abide. The moment this plan goes forth, all other considerations will be laid aside— and the great question will be, shall there be a national government or not?

Benjamin Franklin aimed his remarks directly at Edmund Randolph.

I hope that you will yet lay aside your objections, and, by concurring with your brethren, prevent the great mischief which the refusal of your name may produce.

But Randolph was not moved. Nor were Gerry and Mason. They are men of strong opinion and will not sign what they cannot support. It is not surprising. This is still a young nation. A national political community is only slowly emerging. Even the men who signed the Declaration of Independence and together fought the Revolution were shaped primarily by their experience in local and state politics. Different origins, different interests, different habits of thought make it hard for them to understand each other. Some were strangers when they gathered here, and with distances so great in this country, even the friends among them see each other but rarely. The country is deeply divided over the issues debated here. Go into the streets and taverns and churches. Read the newspapers, pamphlets, and essays, and you will hear the hot words and clashing opinions of a people still trying to decide—what is America, anyway? Many here wish this convention to speak as one. To want such unanimity is understandable. To expect it is . . . a little un-American. And to get it would be a miracle.

The Final Day
(Continued)

L<small>EAVE IT TO</small> Benjamin Franklin to get the first—and last—word on this final day of the convention. He reads this assembly of politicians as if it were an electrical storm, which it has often threatened to be. Doctor Franklin still yearns for unanimity from this convention. It will help to win support for the Constitution in the hard fight for ratification that lies ahead. So he wrote a speech aimed at the doubting Thomases.

> *I confess that there are several parts of this constitution which I do not at present approve, but I am not sure I shall never approve them. For having lived long, I have experienced many instances of being obliged to change opinions even on important subjects.*

Franklin said most people, like most churches, are tempted by notions of their own infallibility. And he warned these men against that common error.

> *I wish that every member of the Convention who may still have objections to the Constitution would with me on this*

occasion doubt a little of his own infallibility—and to make
manifest our unanimity, put his name to this instrument.

This document is not the perfection we once sought,
Franklin told them, but it's the best we could politically expect:

> *It astonishes me to find this system approaching so near*
> *to perfection as it does. Thus I consent, Sir, to this Constitution because I expect no better, and because I am not*
> *sure that it is not the best. I hope that for our own sakes*
> *as part of the people, and for the sake of posterity, we*
> *shall act heartily and unanimously in recommending this*
> *Constitution.*

Franklin then moved that the Constitution be approved
with the "unanimous consent of the States present." Every
state voted "aye," although there were dissenters in some
delegations. One by one, state by state, the delegates came
forward to sign. It's said Franklin wept when his turn came.
As the ink dried on the parchment, the old man turned to the
chair where his friend, George Washington, had presided
over the convention. He looked at the sun painted there and
said that often, during the "vicissitudes" of these debates,
he had wondered whether the sun was rising or setting. Now,
Franklin said, he was sure—quite sure—the sun is rising.

Credits

Executive Producer: Alvin H. Perlmutter

Senior Producer: Christopher Lukas

Producer: Paul Budline

Writers: Paul Budline, Lindsay Miller, Bill Moyers, Andie Tucher

Series Historian: Bernard Weisberger

Associate Producer: Jane Murphy-Schulberg

Graphics Coordinator/Researcher: Elizabeth Fischer

Project Administration: Nancy Pelz-Paget

Historical Consultant: Richard B. Bernstein

Production Executive: Douglas P. Sinsel

Co-Executive Producer: Joan Konner

Executive Editor: Bill Moyers

A Production of: Alvin H. Perlmutter, Inc. and Public Affairs Television, Inc.

The broadcasts of *Moyers: Report from Philadelphia* were made possible by the Corporation for Public Broadcasting, public television stations, and **PaineWebber.**